Conversations with Roger Scruton

Conversations with Roger Scruton

Roger Scruton and Mark Dooley

B L O O M S B U R Y
LONDON · OXFORD · NEW YORK · NEW DELHI · SYDNEY

Bloomsbury Continuum
An imprint of Bloomsbury Publishing Plc

50 Bedford Square
London
WC1B 3DP
UK

1385 Broadway
New York
NY 10018
USA

www.bloomsbury.com

Bloomsbury, Continuum and the Diana logo are trademarks of Bloomsbury Publishing Plc

First published 2016

British Library Cataloguing-in-Publication Data
A catalogue record for this book is available from the British Library.

Library of Congress Cataloguing-in-Publication data has been applied for.

ISBN: HB: 9781472917096
ePDF: 9781472917119
ePub: 9781472917102

2 4 6 8 10 9 7 5 3 1

Printed and bound in Great Britain by CPI Group (UK) Ltd, Croydon CR0 4YY

To find out more about our authors and books visit www.bloomsbury.com.
Here you will find extracts, author interviews, details of forthcoming events
and the option to sign up for our newsletters.

Contents

Preface

These conversations took place over three days in March 2015. They were conducted at Sunday Hill Farm, Roger Scruton's home in Wiltshire. I wish to thank Roger, his wife Sophie ànd their children Sam and Lucy, for their wonderful hospitality during my visit. I am especially grateful to Roger for the time and commitment which he gave this project. I am also thankful to my editors at Bloomsbury, Robin Baird-Smith and Jamie Birkett, for their encouragement and patience.

What follows is a broad-ranging and fairly intimate portrait of Scruton's life and career, one that sheds some new light on both. While the form of the conversations is generally chronological, they often move from biography to ideas and back again. I hope that this will give the reader a greater understanding of Scruton's thought, but also of the unusual life that lies behind it. In the end, however, this book can be summed up by something Scruton said to me shortly after I arrived at Sunday Hill Farm: 'So, Mark, you have come to show the world that I am human!' These conversations testify to the fact that Roger Scruton is indeed both human *and* humorous. And it is he, not me, who shows the world that this is so.

Dublin
November 2015

1

Childhood and Cambridge

'*It was not a happy home*'

I had already published two books on Roger Scruton, dealing with his philosophy, conservatism and his many other interests.[1] This time, however, I was in pursuit of the man behind the work. I wanted Scruton to tell the story of how he became the person that he is. And so I travelled from Dublin to Sunday Hill Farm in Wiltshire, where Roger has lived since 1993. This would not be my first visit to a place to which he has so often and movingly paid tribute in various writings. As you approach Sunday Hill, which sits on the outskirts of Malmesbury, you realize just how apt Scruton's descriptions of his beautiful 'settlement' are. One, in particular, comes to mind each time I spot the farm on the horizon:

> It was thus that … I came to Sunday Hill Farm, bringing with me a library, three pianos and four horses. I was the first 'off-comer' to attempt to settle among families that had farmed here for centuries … Sunday Hill Farm is an old cottage of Cotswold stone, with a stone barn attached to one side of it. My first act on moving in was to replace the metal-framed windows and to cover the grim concrete extension with a veneer of rendering. So far as I could see nobody in the valley had ever before carried out building work for aesthetic reasons. It

was a dangerous thing to do; still more dangerous to pull down three sheds built from panels of some hideous aggregate with an appearance of dried vomit. I was acutely aware of the eyes observing me, of the suppressed indignation at the sight of useful things destroyed, and of the insult to farming implied by my bourgeois need for things to look right, rather than to work right. For my neighbours the landscape was reality – the source of their livelihood, and the recipient of their toil. For me it was appearance – the view from my window, my 'sweet especial rural scene'.[2]

Today, Sunday Hill Farm is very much woven into the fabric of the Wiltshire farmlands. Scruton's attempt to make it 'look right' was in keeping with his conviction, best summed up by Oscar Wilde, that 'it is only shallow people who do not judge by appearances'. The 'old stone barn' has been converted into a library, containing antique furniture and two pianos. It is in this room that Scruton writes, composes and ponders his 'sweet especial rural scene'. His home – which he shares with Sophie and their two children Sam and Lucy – is testimony to Scruton's cultural values, his love of music, his concern for his surroundings and in particular his passion for horses.

People often ask me how I became interested in Roger Scruton. How was it that an Irishman should come to share the vision of the quintessential English conservative? One of the reasons, apart from our shared philosophical outlook, is that my family has long been associated with the horse. My great-grandfather ran a successful stable yard, and it was from there that my grandmother emerged as a horsewoman of some skill. Indeed, she would go on to compete at the highest levels of Irish show jumping. My parents met through show jumping and continue to compete. I, too, competed for many years before taking up a position as commentator on the national show jumping circuit.

When I first encountered Scruton, I was struck by the fact that his life, like mine, had been touched by horses. As he wrote in *On Hunting*:

My life divides into three parts. In the first I was wretched; in the second ill at ease; in the third hunting. Most hunting people are brought up in the sport, and shaped by it into a kind of intermediate species, an ancient synthesis of horse, hound and human. Even now I have the sense of hovering on the periphery of the rite, a fascinated spectator of something which has come into being like a language, to be passed down the generations and absorbed from birth, and which can be learned in later life only at the cost of speaking with a foreign accent.[3]

Unlike Scruton, I was one of those who had been shaped by hunting and show jumping. I was someone who had absorbed from birth the equestrian vernacular of my ancestors. Yet, for all his anxiety, Scruton is certainly no spectator. He is very much at home in the world of horses and has, in turn, given many of them a good home. The home into which I wandered to conduct our conversations is not so much one of books and ideas, although they dominate as much as anything else. It is, if anything, a world where the horse is at home. And, that being the case, so was I.

All aspects of Scruton's thinking are embodied in his homestead and lifestyle. This is a world of farmers and philosophers, of Wagner and wine, of animals and Aristotle. Shortly after I arrive, we are joined by Paddy the dog. Paddy is a black Labrador with big soulful eyes. This is the first time he has been to his new home, and yet it is as though he has been here all his life. Such is the rhythm of life on this farm that those who visit feel as though they have always been part of the routine. As such, Paddy and I settle in seamlessly.

Roger Scruton did not start life this way. His was not a world of horses, scholarship and culture. 'I had a very ordinary childhood,' he exclaims as we sit in his converted barn. We already know from his previous autobiographical statements that Roger Scruton's childhood was, indeed, relatively ordinary. Born to Jack and Beryl on 27 February 1944, he was raised with his two sisters in the town of High Wycombe in Buckinghamshire. As he wrote in *Gentle Regrets: Thoughts from a Life*:

My mother was born and bred in the genteel suburbs of London, cherishing an ideal of gentlemanly conduct and social distinction that my father set out with considerable relish to destroy. She saw in me her great hope of rescue from the Lawrentian wildness of Jack Scruton, and of a return to the quiet tea-parties and box-lined gardens of Upper Norwood. She therefore decided that I should be called Vernon, after a distant cousin who looked sweet and poetic in photographs, but whose greatest merit was that he had emigrated to Canada before he could reveal how few real merits he had. My father, who perhaps saw in this name a fitting revenge for my existence, acquiesced to his wife's desire. However, a residual tenderness towards his son reminded him of the misery that would be faced by a boy with a cissy name, if he could not fight his way to another one. He therefore insisted also on Roger, after Sir Roger de Buslingthorpe, who lay in effigy in the church next to the farm where I was born. Furthermore it was mercifully agreed between my parents that, while I was to be called Vernon by all my relations, Roger would be the first name on my birth certificate and, as it were, the official title that I would one day win through my deeds.[4]

Those deeds would, in time, reward 'Roger' with great fame as a philosopher, writer, journalist and intellectual dissident. As a child, however, he did not have 'those rapturous, Proustian moments in which the whole of one's forthcoming life is condensed'. That was, he believes, because he came from a home where 'there was obviously trouble between my father and my mother of some kind, that we never really fully understood'. There was 'great tension in the household, and the children constantly crept around this tension, afraid of tripping the switch'. The source of that tension was his father, whom Roger describes as 'a ball of electricity that sat silent in the middle of the room'.

Beryl, on the other hand, was 'the mildest and sweetest of people, who would never respond with anger to the anger that she received'. The sad truth was that although the Scruton children loved her dearly, 'we had each grown a carapace against this love, knowing how much it would expose us to his anger'.[5] However, even this protective strategy could not shield Roger from Jack's 'malign energy'. Emerging into self-consciousness 'around the age of six or seven, I became more and more aware that his feelings towards me were not straightforwardly those of a father to a son: there was rivalry and frustration at his own life which continued to accumulate. As a result, I could not say that I had a happy childhood.'

Jack Scruton was the most important influence on the young Roger. He was 'a strong demonic character with a touch of his old Manchester working-class grit. He had very strong beliefs of a socialist, egalitarian kind. These went with a burden of resentment towards the upper classes, something which made him very much of his time. My father was, therefore, the fount of all the ideas and emotions that perambulated in our household.' Conversely, Scruton's mother was a 'gentle, introspective person who was very unconfident in herself'. Unlike Jack, 'not very much came out of her. She was, however, very intelligent and understood what was going on, although she did not want to put herself forward in order to express what she knew.' Was she a source of consolation in the midst of all this anger? 'She was and she wasn't, simply because she was so frightened by it that she couldn't stand up to the real attacks.' Such consolation as the Scruton children had, 'we had in each other. My eldest sister and I were very close and still are. We recognized that we had to shelter each other from the prevailing winds.'

As we talk about this black period in his life, I recall reading previous statements Scruton made about his parents and asking myself why two so seemingly ill-suited people should have got married. When I ask Scruton for an answer to this he is unequivocal: 'They were definitely in love with each other. In those days, people didn't experiment with love. It was either there or not. And when it was, there was courtship, which is something that has disappeared from the world. My father and mother met during the war while serving together in Bomber Command. In the stress of war, two lonely people found companionship in each other. This is a beautiful thing in itself.

'My father, coming from a working-class family with six surviving children out of eight, and a drunken father who terrorized the household, was relieved to get away into the Royal Air Force. My mother, who volunteered during the war, had been put out to grass by her mother after my grandfather died when Beryl was aged just three. Actually she wasn't called Beryl – it was an affected name that she rejected as I had rejected mine. To her friends she was Johnny, and to her children Darl, which had been my father's name for her. Darl's mother felt the need for another husband at all costs, even the cost of discarding her child, which in those days was almost a necessity in the class to which she belonged. And so my mother was brought up by a frozen aunt, a member of the Plymouth Brethren who forbad all toys and jokes and trivia. This meant that my mother's background was also quite intimidating. Consequently, each of my parents – serving in the armed forces in the conditions of war, which automatically creates a sense of the existential importance of everything – discovered a soul mate in the other, a person who would make up for all the love that had been denied to them. Suddenly their loneliness, and the fears instilled by their separate childhoods, seemed as though they had a cure. They did their courting along the banks of the Thames, because that is where the Bomber Command was. They fell in love, not only with each other, but with the banks of the Thames. As soon as he was out of the air force, my father decided he would try to get a job in the High Wycombe area. High Wycombe was not then what it is now: it was not a messy suburb of London. It was a piece of old England, and the idea of old England deeply touched my father, partly because old England hovered so near to his eyes in this Southern landscape, but also just out of reach, the upper classes having stolen it, and furnished it for their exclusive use.'

Our conversation is interrupted by Sam, who has made me a sandwich. Sam is joyful, outgoing and confident. You can see that he is very much at home on Sunday Hill Farm. As Roger congratulates his son on his sandwich-making skills, I am struck by just how different all this is to the household in which Sam's father grew up. Scruton has a profound love for his children, something I would recognize more and more as the days progressed. He is an affectionate and caring father, someone who stands in complete contrast to the fraught and frustrated man we are discussing. Still, as Sam departs with a smile from his dad, I get a sense that Jack's love of old England was something admired by Scruton. After all, his book *England: An Elegy* is a tribute to precisely this idea.[6]

This leads me to ask if Jack was someone like George Orwell, a man of the old left who, unlike those on the postmodern left, loved his country, its institutions and its role in the world. Could this be a sort of spiritual common ground upon which the angst of childhood might be laid to rest? 'My father was a little bit like Orwell, although he was not an educated man. He did a crash course in teacher training after the war, when those crash courses were available for ex-servicemen. As a result he was able to teach in a primary school, but he didn't have the qualifications required to move up in the profession. Hence, he remained always at the bottom. That very much enhanced his resentment, because he knew that he had intellectual gifts. But he had no instruction. This was very difficult for him to cope with: he suffered his situation in the same spirit as Jude the Obscure.

'On the other hand, he had that old Orwellian patriotism which set him at odds with Marxism – a kind of leftist thinking which, in so far as he understood it, he hated. He also hated communism. He wanted an England that would be both socialist *and* England. However, his idea of England was distorted by the fact that he couldn't cope with religion. His mother had brought him up in the Anglican Church, which is very odd for someone from the slums of Manchester, although an astute calculation on his mother's part, since she rightly saw the Anglican Church as a way to climb the social ladder. Unfortunately this apprenticeship in social climbing had exactly the wrong effect on Jack, who forever afterwards saw the Anglican Church as a symbol of the old class hierarchies. That is why he insisted we go to a suitably gloomy, non-conformist chapel. Not, of course, that he ever believed in what was preached there – he was an atheist through and through. God too was a member of the upper-class conspiracy. But he would inspect our local chapels and, if they seemed suitably cold and forbidding, tell us "that's where you have got to go every Sunday!"'

What of Scruton's mother, was she in any way religious? 'No. She was totally commonsensical. Her thought was "if God existed, he would not have permitted that war. And since the war occurred, God doesn't exist." When I laugh and comment that she sounded like Stephen Fry, her son responds: 'It's a very respectable attitude!' However, 'she was glad we went to the Baptist Chapel and it was something she didn't discourage. What she didn't know, however, was that I went in secret to the Anglican Church.

My mother was typical of her generation. As Orwell said and as Hume had said two centuries before, the English don't have any religion. They were very religious in the seventeenth century, when they killed each other by the thousands. That experience cured them of religion, persuaded them that it is not for this kind of thing that England exists. Ever since the Glorious Revolution, the expulsion of James II and the bringing in of that dreary old king from Holland, there has been a sense that we've done religion and need only adhere to the forms. Life is too short to bother with the doctrines. I think that this attitude became much more pronounced in the twentieth century, which is what Orwell was highlighting when he said that, although the English have no religious belief, they have a strong sense of what is and is not correct. I would add they also have a longing for enchantment, provided it is of an unthreatening and home-made kind.'

These are points that Scruton has recently discussed in *England: An Elegy* and *Our Church: A Personal History of the Church of England.*[7] But surely, by sneaking off to the Anglican Church behind his parents' back, he had a more exalted idea of religion and its role in society? 'Yes. I was enthralled by the ceremony, the sense of holiness, the music, the choir. Earlier I had even sung in the church choir at High Wycombe, since that was part of our music classes in primary school. I was fascinated by the idea that you could do this thing properly, and not just guiltily. I guess the Anglican Church already was for me a symbol of my country. I inherited from my father a love of England as a moral idea, and like him I saw that this moral idea has an aesthetic expression. You see, although atheism was quite an important part of my father's makeup, England was an *enchanted* place for him. Coming from the slums of Manchester down to the Thames Valley, as it then was, he was granted a kind of revelation of what had grown and flourished here, and what had made this place unique. And the fact that he and my mother, along with all their friends and neighbours, were fighting for it enhanced that feeling. After the war he took out a subscription to *The Countryman* magazine that H. J. Massingham wrote for. Massingham, a guild socialist with Christian leanings, conveyed to my father a sense of the immemorial rhythm of the English landscape, and the way in which it had been built by human hands and rustic labour.'

I draw the conclusion that Jack Scruton could have done much more with his life than he did, or, indeed, was permitted to. After all, someone who thought so deeply about his country and its place in the world, someone who had reflected so hard on religion, was obviously destined for more than the life that Jack had chosen to lead. Had he desired to do so, could he have progressed further? Scruton believes he possibly could have, although 'he had great trouble with his profession because he didn't suffer fools gladly, and the fools were always in a position superior to him. He would have loved to be headmaster at one of our little village schools, such as the one at Ibstone, one of many beautiful little villages in our neighbourhood. However, they were Church of England schools, and when you applied for a job you had to fill in the section that asked for your religion. And because he always wrote "Atheist" in huge letters, he had no chance of being given the job! It was admirable in a way, but also very self-destructive.'

Surrounded by all this darkness, frustration and resentment, did Scruton enjoy any happiness? Were there any sources of consolation in an otherwise oppressive household? 'No. Not really. My father became violent at a certain stage and, looking back on it, I think he must have had some sort of depression. So it was not a happy home. I actually ran away when I was seventeen, just after I had finished the Cambridge scholarship exams. I lived on the floor of my sister's boyfriend's room in Mile End Road, and survived by washing up in the Lyons Corner House in Leadenhall Street. They don't have Corner Houses any more ...' Scruton lived on that floor for a few months before hitch-hiking to Greece with a school friend.

Before we leave Jack and Beryl (aka Johnny) behind, I am curious about Scruton's childhood heroes. Were there any people outside the home, whether in high or popular culture, that inspired him to follow the path he eventually took? 'I was very studious and I worked very hard at school, especially at the natural sciences, which were my A-Level subjects. However, I discovered literature, music and art, and everything changed for me as a result. We moved to Marlow to be near my mother's mother, who lived there. And in Marlow at that time, there were some quite interesting people. I got to know one family in particular. The girls, Bron – who was actually my first girlfriend – and Francesca, were at the high school. Their mother Isabel had been married to Desmond Ryan, whom I describe in my book *I Drink Therefore I Am: A Philosopher's Guide to Wine*.'

Scruton's memorable description of his friend, Desmond Ryan, occurs in the opening chapter of that book, suitably titled 'My Fall'. He writes: 'I drank without knowledge, ignorant of the priests that Bacchus had spread around our world, and who pursue their calling in places which can be discovered by accident but seldom by design.' All that changed, however, when

> [d]uring my summer vacations from Cambridge I sometimes stayed with Desmond, a witty Irishman who had read everything, slept with everyone, spent whatever he could, and was recovering in a village near Fontainebleau. It took a little time to discover that Desmond was an ordained priest of Bacchus, since his doctor had advised restraint in the matter of alcohol. Desmond had interpreted this to mean first-growth clarets at dinner, and maybe second-growth at lunch. His doctor, he felt certain, would particularly approve of the Château Trotanoy 1945, made from the last grapes to escape the plague of phylloxera, which had such an improving effect on a frail constitution when drunk alone after dinner. Desmond held that such wines would be quite insulting to the medical condition of his young guest, whose untutored taste-buds and anaemic bloodstream were clearly crying out for Beaujolais. I gratefully drank what was offered, and felt sorry for Desmond, that his life was so bound by dreary medicinal routines.[8]

That a fellow Irishman should have introduced Roger Scruton to fine French wine was, for me, a glorious revelation.

By the time Scruton met Isabel, she had left Desmond and was 'living with a guy called Bob Newman, an American abstract painter, who had been a friend of Hemingway and had written various Hemingway-like novels. That family was through and through bohemian, living from hand to mouth, in a big house at the end of our road, overlooking the garden of another big house occupied by the ageing Scott Moncrieff, translator of Proust. They were people of the kind who inherit fortunes, spend them in a couple of weeks and then live in absolute poverty until the next fortune comes along, which generally it does.

'I also had a close relationship with a boy called John Law. I had friends in our grammar school but the friend who mattered most to me was one who existed outside my circle there. John was the product of a local "secondary-modern" school, which is to say that he had failed to pass the 11-plus examination that would have permitted him to go to the grammar school. He was much older than me, in his early twenties, while I was sixteen. He was an orphan, a "Barnardo's boy", who had been adopted by an elderly local couple to whom he had never taken, and to whom he rarely returned from his adventures on the edge of things. He lived as an outsider and a reject, cadging bed and board where he could, trusting in nothing other than his artistic talent (he painted, fearsome abstracts in oils, which soon gave way to strangely haunting mobiles that he would dangle from the ceiling in whatever house he had briefly found shelter). His extraordinary enthusiasm was contagious, and he introduced me to Colin Wilson's book *The Outsider*, which was his guide to life. He would treat me, when we met, to long monologues of rapture on the subject of Van Gogh, Matisse, Léger and Maillol, whose work he was studying at Corsham College of Art. From John, who was a solipsist who cared for no one but sought attention from everyone, I learned that nothing really matters except art. Everything else is phoney.'

However, the 'biggest single influence' on the young Scruton were the letters of Rainer Maria Rilke. When his parents decided they wanted to purchase a particular property in Marlow, the owners, 'a retired couple called Deas who were emigrating to Canada, drove over to discuss the deal. I was left sitting in the same spot in our garden [on Amersham Road], drinking tea with their son.' Scruton's description of their son, Ivor Deas, is a nice illustration of his literary talent:

I had heard rumours of the artistic temperament, and something about Ivor Deas made me suspect he suffered from this obscure but distinguished ailment. He was a bachelor of some 40 years, still living with his parents. His face was pale and thin, with grey eyes that seemed to fade away when you looked at them. His alabaster hands with their long white fingers; his quiet voice; his spare and careful words; his trousers, rubbed shiny at the knees; and his Adam's apple shifting up and down like a ping-pong ball in a fountain – all these seemed totally out of place in our suburb and conferred on him an air of suffering fragility that must surely have some literary cause. He sat in silence, waiting for me to speak. I asked him his occupation. He responded with an embarrassed laugh. 'Librarian,' he said, and I looked at him amazed.[9]

The deal was settled and Ivor was rushed from the garden by his mother, 'a large formidable-looking lady, with permed grey hair and layers of woollen clothing in maroon and mauve'. However, because Ivor's books could not be taken to Canada without causing the family 'to go over the weight limit', his parents asked Jack and Beryl if they could leave them behind. And the first book that Roger picked from Ivor's collection was Rilke's letters. In the opening pages of *Gentle Regrets*, he beautifully describes that moment:

Needless to say, I had never heard of this writer, but I was attracted by his name. 'Rainer' had a faraway, exotic sound to it; 'Rilke' suggested knighthood and chivalry. And 'Maria' made me think of a being more spiritual than material, who had risen so high above the scheme of things as no longer to possess a sex. I read the book with a feeling of astonishment, just as I had experienced two years before through Bunyan. An air of sanctity, a reckless disregard for the world and its requirements, seemed to radiate from those mysterious pages. Here was a man who wandered outside society, communicating with nature and his soul. I did not suspect that Rilke was a shameless sponge; I could not see that these letters, which seem to be all giving, are in fact all taking, the work of a spiritual vampire. To me they exemplified another, higher mode of being, of which I had no precise conception, but for which I tried to find a name: 'aesthetic' sounded right at first; but then 'ascetic' seemed just as good, and somewhat easier to say. Eventually I used both words interchangeably, satisfied that between them they captured the mysterious vision that had been granted to me, but withheld from those coarser beings – my parents and sisters, for instance – who had no knowledge of books.[10]

Those letters, he tells me, 'made a huge impression'. But so, too, did the 'little volumes of Dante, which all seemed so mysterious and full of meaning. That was when I decided I must be a writer.'

Before that pivotal moment, when he discovered his calling, there must have been other interests in Scruton's life, such as sport or popular culture? 'I hated sport. We had television but were forbidden to watch it, and I did play guitar. Later at Cambridge, we formed a little group and I played pop music. I even played trombone in a little band at a certain stage. I regarded all that as amusing and fun, but nothing to do with real music.' Did this teenage boy really know the distinction between real music and all the rest? 'I *totally* knew the distinction! I *always* knew it. It was absolutely clear to me, although I couldn't have put it into words. There was real art, on the one hand, and there was the kind of crap my sisters were addicted to on the other!'

But where did that ability to discern between the real and the fake come from? 'I don't know. It was, I suppose, partly the influence of John Law and his view that nothing matters except art – for if that is true, popular culture, which matters not a jot, could not be art. But there was the indirect influence of the Leavisite schoolteacher, Mr Broadbridge, under whose spell I fell while at High Wycombe Royal Grammar School. Although I never met him, I felt his influence through my school friends who were studying A-Level English. The Leavisite movement was very strong in the schools back then, because it gave teachers something to cling to. Literature was taught in our school as a form of judgement and not as a form of enjoyment. This was something that hit me straight away at that turning point in my life between fifteen and sixteen – it was simply obvious that art, music and literature are serious in a way that science could never be.'

However, I want to know if, in such a home, Scruton had any exposure to 'real music' before this crucial turning point. As if recalling some long-forgotten but precious memory, he says: 'I must have been thirteen when my father's mother died, and her effects were inherited by the various children. Her piano came to us, a little upright of the kind described by D. H. Lawrence in "Piano", a poem that evokes the old working-class way of life that my father had known, and for which he sometimes wept in the way that Lawrence describes. Anyway, this piano had been at the centre of the household in Capel Street, Ancoats, and had been played by my father's favourite sister, who died aged eighteen of TB. It was, therefore, a precious object to him. It wasn't a great piano, but when it arrived from Manchester it was the first time there had been a musical instrument in the home. Our mother, much to our common surprise, sat at it and played things she had learned as a child, such as the slow movement of Beethoven's Pathétique Sonata. She could only do the top two voices, but I thought the piece was so beautiful and extraordinary. I had sung in the choir at school and in our local church before my voice broke – this being a permitted contact with the Anglican mystery since, after all, singing is not believing (a view that I came to doubt in time). I knew what music was. But I had never been moved by it like that before. Then we acquired an old wind-up gramophone with some seventy-eight RPM records. Our first records were *The Thieving Magpie* overture by Rossini, Mozart's *Eine Kleine Nachtmusik* and Mendelssohn's *Hebrides Overture*. These had a *huge* impact, and especially the contrapuntal development of the Mendelssohn, which made it clear that music is a kind of argument from premise to conclusion and not just something to be enjoyed. I then joined something called The Classics Club, which sent out pirated editions through the post. I built up a small collection of records: *The Planets*, Tchaikovsky and Haydn symphonies and so on.'

Did the young Scruton listen to these alone or did he have company in this new mysterious world? 'Mostly alone, because no one else was really interested. But through a music society at school I made musical friends. Everything moved so quickly back then. As soon as you discovered something, you very quickly discovered someone else who was also interested in it, and you went on to share and to amplify your interest. That is because there weren't any distractions. Boys weren't going around looking at their smart-phones, and if they were thinking of girls it was not of the girl at the front of the class, since ours was a boys' school. We were all eager to find somebody with whom to share an interest. I became friendly with a contemporary named Dave Cox, who was younger than me but who could really play the piano. And we egged each other on to know everything about music. I had some piano lessons, but my father took a turn against it and prevented me from continuing. Despite that, I learned to sight-read and Dave and I used to play duets together – including the four-hand version of the *Rite of Spring*, with which we entertained our schoolfellows at lunch-time on the school piano.'

A new world had suddenly opened up to Scruton, a vision of the human condition that would, one day, become his primary preoccupation. But which of the great cultural figures first captivated this young boy who was now settled in Marlow, and who was, slowly but surely, discovering that there is much more to life than the socialist ideals of his father? 'Bartók, Stravinsky, T. S. Eliot, Robert Graves up to a point – *The White Goddess* had a big impact – and, of course, Rilke. It was all very modern – a collection of whispering voices that my parents could not hear.'

All of this happened while Scruton was at the Royal Grammar School, but did he like school? 'Not really, because by the time I started moving in this artistic direction, I was committed to doing the A-Level sciences and I began to feel that I was studying the wrong things. That said, I did well at A-Level and got into Cambridge.' So why, with such an artistic temperament, did he opt to study the sciences? 'This was the time when people thought that children should be studying sciences, because that is where the future lies. The view of people like my parents was: what's the point in studying Greek and Latin? All my subsequent thoughts about education have been an answer to that question. I was from an early age a convert to the view that the only really useful subjects are studies of the useless. But at the time I could not put this into practice since I was dependent on others' decisions in the matter. I so regretted not studying Greek and had to teach myself later. How could I be a philosopher and Greekless?'

An obviously gifted and exceptional student, did Scruton feel that he was outgrowing school? 'Oh definitely, but I wasn't the only one. There was a circle of us that moved away from it. We weren't really there. But we would meet in the evening to discuss things, sometimes in the pubs (pubs in those days did not have idiot music played at full volume), and sometimes in our homes.' Did this lead to a certain disdain for the educational establishment? 'Interestingly enough, I didn't think in terms of an "educational establishment". I was lucky being at that beautiful grammar school, because all the teaching that came in my direction came from individual people who had something to say, and were essentially mentors. I have described in many contexts my beloved physics master, Guy Chapman.[11] There was also my chemistry master, Denis Pelmore, who had a lot of poetry in him, and who introduced me to Heine and the German romantics (he had been stationed in Germany after the war, and taken the experience seriously). The music master, James Swinnerton Dawes – Jackdaw, as we called him – was a friend of the composer Edmund Rubbra, who lived nearby. Such people were enormous presences in the school, and the school was unimportant in comparison with them. They were people whose interest was interest. If they found a boy who was interested in something, they would at once leap in to welcome him into the realm of knowledge.'

I interject to enquire how such men might view the state of education today. 'I think they'd commit suicide! Things were much easier for them then because, first of all, they had a boys' school which modelled itself on a public school – on Eton in fact – and for the most part they had been educated in such a school themselves. There was very strict discipline, including corporal punishment. So boys did not misbehave. I did, but most didn't.' And did the mischievous young Scruton get beaten for his efforts? 'Yes, of course.'

There were also 'many clubs and societies' in the school. 'We had our school orchestra, performed plays and each year a Gilbert and Sullivan opera. Culture was absolutely integral to the education that we were offered. Moreover we were always pushed forward to the next stage from the one we had got to. We learned things at school that you don't even get at university now. In scholarship-level mathematics, we worked right through Piaggio's book on differential equations, which is really difficult stuff and necessary for physics. Today, people don't get anywhere near that until at least their second year in university.'

I ask Scruton, as a father who attends his son's school performances, whether his parents ever came to see him perform. 'No, I was a bone of contention. When I became interested in music I wanted to learn the cello, and there was a school cello that I was able to borrow for my lessons. But our household budget was very constrained, and my musical education not in any way high on my father's agenda. So when we moved away from the school to Marlow I had to give up the cello.'

The picture he paints is that of a studious, introverted boy who found solace in culture and academic achievement. Yet, there was also a naughty and playful side to Scruton's character: 'Oh yes! You see, I had many friends and we did lots of things together, and some of these *were* naughty. Because of my scientific training I became interested in explosives and I used to blow things up. I became quite expert in this. Probably because of my difficult home life, I was a troublemaker who was ill at ease. It wasn't that I wanted to destroy things, but I did want to put down a marker for the different vision of life that I imagined myself to have, in comparison with all those normal people around me. Some would say that that has remained as a feature of my personality, though of course I would vigorously deny it, and my conservatism is in part a way of denying it. At a certain stage, partly because of knowing Bob Newman, Isabel, Bron and Francesca, I wanted to be like them. I wanted to live my life in the style of the Left Bank in Paris. Not that I had ever been to Paris, but I had an idea of it, and ideas are so much more potent than realities. Bob's stories of evenings in 'La Coupole' on the Boulevard Montparnasse, when Milhaud, Hemingway, Prévert and sometimes even Picasso would drop in, overwhelmed me with desire for this enchanted world that lay just a few hundred miles away across the water.

'So yes, I was perfectly happy not to fit in. I regarded myself as a misfit. I was a romantic and a bohemian, and I loved my circle of friends. We entertained ourselves by talking about literature and music, and sometimes by playing music. I had a friend who was *really* musical and who lived down the road with his very musical family. He and I played through all the difficult piano repertoire, he taking one hand and I taking the other. All of us used to write poems and stories too, and I still have some of them.'

Was Scruton just drifting at this early stage or did he have some definite ambitions? 'No, but I had some *indefinite* ambitions – namely, to be some kind of intellectual figure. I wanted to write and to think…' But surely he had some definite academic ambitions? 'When given a task I want to succeed at it. So, I was given the task of doing my A-Levels and getting to Cambridge. Therefore, I did my A-Levels and got to Cambridge, but it wasn't as though *that* was my ambition. Once at Cambridge, the task was to get a good degree, so I got a good degree.' I press Scruton to find out when, precisely, he embarked on an academic career. 'After I got to Cambridge I changed subjects from sciences to philosophy – which was called "Moral Sciences" in those days. There was a lot of empirical psychology in it, in fact. I then became fascinated by philosophy and by the intellectual life. I read what I was supposed to read, I did my weekly essay and, as always, I wanted to do it well. So I did it well and I got a good degree. But during the course of this, I sometimes asked myself "where am I going?" And always the answer would be that I must be a writer – that is the thing I *must* be. I thought I must write a novel, I must write some poems, I must write some essays. But I couldn't do any of those things! I was convulsed with a sense of my impotence and unimportance. However, I didn't regard the academic life either as natural for me or as the inevitable alternative to being a writer.

'I sometimes sought advice from tutors and others, but they didn't really have much to say. So I left Cambridge when I got my degree, and I didn't arrange to do research or anything like that. I decided that I should go out into the world, try my fortunes and perhaps *be* this bohemian thing that I had for so long wanted to be. So I left university with the intention of being a writer and I tried to survive for two difficult years with a pen in my hand. During that time my mother fell ill with what was to become terminal cancer. I also met Danielle, my first wife, while teaching as *lecteur* in the Collège Universitaire at Pau in the Pyrenees. I came home from Pau to look after my mother, but the situation at home was by then impossible. I could not share the house with my father, whose anger had amplified in ways that I would never have foreseen – as though I was to blame for my mother's impending death. I had to escape, and went to stay in the forest of Fontainebleau with Desmond, whose loving nature I had always relied on. But of course, knowing that my mother was dying without me caused paroxysms of guilt that stayed with me thereafter – something that I describe in the chapter of *Gentle Regrets* titled 'Growing up with Sam', which in my view is one of the best things I have written.[12] I came back when my mother was dying, and said farewell to this poor woman who had never known, because we could not express it, how much her children loved her, and who had been too shy and intimidated to ask. After she died, I went to Italy, and stayed the rest of that year in Rome.'

As I sit in his study surrounded by thousands of books, I realize that Scruton's life as a philosopher may have happened by chance. He wanted to be a writer but had no means of support. Was it that a career in academia might provide him with the resources and the space required to be the writer he wished to be? Or was it that, along with novels, essays and poetry, he also wanted to write philosophy? I ask him if he read any philosophy at school. 'I read Bertrand Russell and Nietzsche. I also read Sartre's *Being and Nothingness*, which I bought from our local bookshop with my pocket money. Our local bookseller was a paraplegic. His jerky movements conferred an air of intellectual distinction, and elicited the greatest respect from us. The respect was reciprocated, since he was impressed by the fact that young boys would order difficult books of whose importance he was one of the few in our town to be aware. A few years after I bought the Sartre the poor man killed himself, unable to bear any longer the physical pain of his condition.

'When the Sartre arrived I couldn't understand it. Nietzsche was, however, a revelation. The first book of his I read was *Thus Spoke Zarathustra*, and that really impressed me because of the passion with which it was written, and for a while I took Nietzsche's diatribes against pity very seriously. But it was our bookseller who cured me. I was looking from a classroom window at school, and caught sight of him as he struggled from his car with a pile of books for the library, and limped towards the entrance, wincing with pain. I was shocked at myself for feeling such pity for him, but sensed also how wrong Nietzsche was about pity, since what I felt was admiration too.

'While I respected those works of philosophy, they didn't really grab me in the way that poetry, prose and novels had grabbed me. And so philosophy was *not* my first choice when I came to Cambridge. I would have preferred to do something difficult like Chinese, but I was put off that by my tutor, who was himself a Chinese scholar. I describe my encounter with this tutor – Lawrence Picken – in *I Drink Therefore I Am*, since he was one of the 'priests of Bacchus' who initiated me into my enduring devotion.'

Scruton is a man who has dedicated his life to philosophy. Initially, however, it was not something that 'grabbed' him. At what point *did* it begin to take hold of him? 'During my first year at Cambridge, I gradually got taken up by analytic philosophy.' How did that happen? 'It happened simply by doing my weekly essay and by going to lectures, which, incidentally, were not very good. I had a terrible tutor, A. C. Ewing, who was senile. However, I became friends with another boy there, Malcolm Budd, who was my contemporary. He had just changed from mathematics to philosophy and had discovered Wittgenstein, with whom he became obsessed. And so we educated each other.' Like Scruton, Malcolm Budd would go on to become one of the most distinguished aestheticians in Britain. He is currently Emeritus Grote Professor of the Philosophy of Mind and Logic at the University of London, a position formerly held by Richard Wollheim and Ted Honderich. As students at Cambridge, however, Scruton and Budd 'dispensed with the whole system by giving each other tutorials'.

Scruton pauses to tell me that he chose to go to Cambridge because 'my school had a connection with Jesus College and quite a lot of us got in. In those days, you were allowed to have special connections. Nowadays, I suppose it would be regarded as unfair. So that is where I ended up. I had been squatting in Birmingham over the summer. I spent my days in the Birmingham City Library. So when I got to Cambridge it was nice to have a room of my own, although it was in other respects quite an ordeal. I didn't fit in among the boys from public schools, since I had the grammar school complex, exacerbated by my spell of homelessness. I was also in a very cold building, the Waterhouse Building in Jesus College, which was a Victorian gothic structure with draughty staircases. I later came to admire Waterhouse, as an architect and painter who had set out to beautify the country that he loved, and from the aesthetic point of view there is no doubt that his building, perfunctory though it may be, is immeasurably superior to the ghastly modernist contraption that was subsequently dumped beside it – though I was the first to move into that contraption when it was built, longing by then for the comforts and contrivances of modernity. But Waterhouse's building was really very forbidding as a place to live. It was 1963, the coldest winter on record. Everything froze and there was no heating. Britain was undergoing the full socialist experience at the time anyway, so nothing worked, there was no electricity and everyone was on strike. Jesus College was therefore not a home from home – rather a new and quixotic way of being homeless.'

As he speaks about Cambridge, I think of Scruton's mother and how proud she must have been to see him succeed against all the odds, not least of which was his father. 'I am sure she was proud,' he says, 'but I am also certain she was never allowed to express it.' And what of Jack – did he ever express any pride that his son had made it to Cambridge? 'Not to me. I think he would always boast about his children to his mates. But I think it was just too painful for him to observe my uninterrupted progress, whereas he had fought at every point to improve his lot and had never succeeded. I wanted him to feel happy and to accept that I was getting on, but he couldn't.'

Did Scruton arrive in Cambridge armed with conservative political convictions? 'No. I suppose I had fairly standard Labour Party views about things. Neither did I think too much about the political direction of my country – that is for sure. I became more and more interested in culture, rather than politics, as the expression of the public life. And there was a vivid idea of culture propagated in Cambridge at the time. Leavis was still alive, pottering in a slightly mad way around the streets of the city. His talks would be given in private rooms and he would carry about with him little bits of paper, which he would unfold in front of his eyes and read in disjointed sentences, as though they were dispatches just received from the Almighty. It was a paranoid performance, but it conveyed a strong sense that Cambridge had once stood for something, had indeed stood in judgement on the national culture. Likewise, it had stood for something in philosophy because of Wittgenstein and Russell, and also of course in mathematics and the sciences. So one was aware of being in the centre of intellectual life, but also aware that, somehow, that life had died. Some traces of those achievements remained, but they were essentially beyond the point of renewal. Those, like the philosopher John Wisdom, who tried to keep the Wittgenstein image alive, were not really persuasive.'

Scruton moved to Moral Sciences in his first year at Cambridge, partly because 'I couldn't imagine anything more boring than having to sit through lectures on crystallography!' That was not the only reason. Having secured a place at Cambridge two years before he could actually attend lectures, he had 'read the books that I was supposed to study in my first year – books on molecular biology and physical chemistry. True, I was fascinated by those subjects, but there was no point in going to lectures that would be simply repeating what I had learned. I don't think this was arrogance on my part. But I couldn't drum up any reserve of interest, and was acutely aware of things going on all around that presented opportunities that it would be crazy not to take. I very much regret that I didn't keep all my science books – I had collected quite a few by then. At a certain stage of revulsion, I just took them along to the second-hand bookshop and dumped them there. I would love to consult them again and to revive some of the scientific knowledge that I then had.'

It strikes me that his early scientific training may have sown the seeds for Scruton's powerful critique of scientism and neurobiology, which feature in so many of his subsequent philosophical writings. A typical example of how he approaches this question is found in *Philosophy: Principles and Problems*:

> Science is a voyage of discovery, which passes from the observed to the unobserved, and thence to the unobservable. Its concepts and theories describe a reality so remote from the world of appearance that we can hardly envisage it, and while its findings are *tested* through observation, this is no more than a trivial consequence of the fact that observation is what 'testing' means. Science explains the appearance of the world, but does not describe it ... Science begins when we ask the

question 'Why?' It leads us from the observed event to the laws which govern it, and onwards to higher and more general laws. But where does the process end? If each new answer prompts another question, then scientific explanations are either incomplete or endless (which is just another way of being incomplete). But in that case science leaves at least one question unanswered. We still don't know why the series of causes exists: the why of this event may be found in that; but what of the why of the world? Cosmologists dispute over the 'origins of the universe', some arguing for a Big Bang, others for a slow condensation. But in the nature of the case, such theories leave a crucial question unanswered. Even if we conclude that the universe began at a certain time from nothing, there is something else that needs to be explained, namely, the 'initial conditions' which then obtained. Something was true of the universe at time zero, namely, that *this* great event was about to erupt into being, and to generate effects in accordance with laws that were already, at this initial instant, sovereign. And what is the why of *that*? A positivist would dismiss such a question as meaningless. So too would many scientists. But if the only grounds for doing so is that science cannot answer it, then the response is self-serving. *Of course* the question has no scientific answer: it is the question beyond science, the question left over when all of science has been written down. It is a philosophical question.[13]

'Yes, I think you are right: my scientific training was very important for this, but not as important as getting through my apprenticeship in analytical philosophy. People outside that discipline don't realize how extraordinary an education analytical philosophy is. I did two years of philosophy without opening a book written before 1900. I knew that there was this guy called Descartes, and I had heard of Kant, but the way that we did philosophy then was purely intellectual, addressing questions and trying to understand them. Your weekly essay might ask you to explore the meaning of 'if' in a subjunctive conditional. That is a really interesting question! "If he *were* to be six foot tall, then she *would* marry him" – what is the force of that and how would you represent it formally? And what is the role of such conditionals in the statement of a scientific theory, because scientific theories *are* counterfactual, otherwise they couldn't be tested? You were confronted with an intellectual problem detached from any history. Neither was it a literary question: getting clear about counterfactuals was as much an intellectual achievement as proving something in maths. As with all philosophical questions, in the end you run out of answers. But that discipline implanted in me a sense of the distinction between real thinking and fake thinking.'

In time, Scruton would cultivate a much more comprehensive philosophical outlook than the purely analytic approach taught at Cambridge. Still, I am interested in finding out who were his teachers at this early stage of his university training. 'That's the big question! My first teacher, as I mentioned earlier, was A. C. Ewing, who was a kind of relic of Edwardian England. He wrote a little book on Kant, and also a big book on idealism. But something had gone: he was senile and his students were desperate to escape him. The college couldn't get rid of him and, as Director of Studies, he would appoint himself as our tutor. Eventually we were assigned a secret tutor who came from London, but who was also nothing special. As a result, Malcolm Budd and I decided that we would teach each other. Malcolm was my first real teacher of philosophy and I was his, and we indelibly marked each other's minds. Then, I managed to get supervision from the philosopher of language Jonathan Bennett. But most of my supervisions during all my time in Cambridge were begged from people. On the other hand, there was, as Ezra Pound would say, a "live tradition" in Cambridge inherited from Russell, Wittgenstein and G. E. Moore, and this entered our thinking by osmosis, enabling us to see how exactly we should approach the questions that had influenced those great minds.'

How, then, did he manage to marry his love of culture with the philosophical insights he was picking up at Cambridge? 'After my two years away, I hadn't succeeded in becoming a writer or anything else from which I could build a career. Partly out of cowardice, and partly out of a sense that my education was incomplete, I went back to Cambridge to do postgraduate research in philosophy. I was accepted straight away and awarded a grant. I then had to choose a topic and I chose aesthetics, thinking that this would, at least, help me to synthesize my interest in philosophy with those artistic aspirations that I was still clinging to. As an undergraduate I had attended some inspiring lectures on aesthetics by Michael Tanner, who was a big influence on all of us. He was slightly outside of the analytical norm, being a Leavisite, a Nietzschean and a passionate Wagnerian. So he would imbue his lectures with references to these other things, which made aesthetics seem exceedingly interesting, a kind of door out of analytic philosophy into the true life of the mind.

'Malcolm, who was then a fellow at Peterhouse, introduced me to the famous little articles on aesthetic concepts by Frank Sibley, which deeply impressed me. I thought this is a *real* topic about which I ought to write a thesis. So I went to see Sibley in Lancaster, thinking I would study with him and get away from Cambridge, the atmosphere of which I had never really liked. But Sibley was a deeply depressed man who wasn't able to elicit much enthusiasm in me since he contained none in himself. I had no choice, therefore, but to stay at Cambridge and to go to Michael Tanner. But for all his great intelligence Tanner seemed unable or unwilling to guide my studies. His rooms in Corpus Christi College were piled high to the ceiling with books. Having tunnelled through to where he was, you would be greeted by the command, "Listen to this!" He would put a record on the gramophone and sway backwards and forwards in ecstasy, indicating by movements of his facial muscles that you were being confronted with the deep meaning of it all. But what that meaning was remained unspoken.'

It becomes clear that Scruton is a philosopher who is almost totally self-taught. He became friends with the English scholar John Casey, who shared similar interests. 'Casey was a very difficult and domineering person. However, partly because of that, I learned a lot from him, and he focused me on what to read. He also had very strong views about literature and criticism, as well as politics. However, although he had a philosophical mind, he was not a philosopher. Eventually, when I was finally given a supervisor, it was Elizabeth Anscombe. But she would only give me tutorials if I provided a bottle of claret and a Havana cigar! There was no way I could go to her with an essay and ask her to look at it for me. So, yes, I am as near as can be to someone who is self-taught, but self-taught through osmosis. I was standing in the shallows of a withdrawing tide. Cambridge was flowing away into the past, but I could absorb through my feet whatever of it remained.'

It is obvious that Scruton absorbed a lot of Wittgenstein. He returns continually to the latter's 'private language' argument throughout his writings, most notably in *Philosophy: Principles and Problems*, where he argues that, in providing the 'decisive refutation' to the Cartesian picture, Wittgenstein 'changed the course of modern philosophy'.[14] He tells me that in his first two years at Cambridge, 'Wittgenstein dominated my thinking'. Then, however, the thinker with whom Scruton is most identified, and whom he admires above all, came into focus: 'Jonathan Bennett was then lecturing on and writing his first book about Kant – *Kant's Analytic*.[15] He was totally enthusiastic about his subject. He was wrestling with Kant and it was a wonderful experience to attend his lectures, which were lectures *to* Kant, and *at* Kant, not merely lectures about him. Looking back on it, I am sure – I *know* – that he misrepresented so much, but he still made Kant alive and present in the room. After that, I set up a little network of other students who were studying Kant, and, once again, we used to teach ourselves and to write essays for each other. I read Kant's *Critique of Pure Reason* about ten times and really got to know it. It sunk into my way of thinking, but did not click until much later. I was then able to write my little book on Kant.'

Scruton's book on Kant was first published in 1982 in the Modern Masters series by Oxford University Press. It is now regarded by many as the definitive introduction to this notoriously complex thinker. This not least because it conveys with admirable clarity the exquisite subtleties of Kant's thought. Scruton comments: 'I suppose it is as clear as anything else written on Kant. And that is because Kant's thinking had filtered down into the heart of me. So yes, he has been the greatest of my philosophical influences. Over the years, however, Hegel also had an impact. I actually found Hegel pretentious and absurd for a long time, but I think it was John Casey, who was then reading Alexandre Kojève's *Introduction to the Reading of Hegel*, who first made me recognize the importance of Hegel. He suggested that I read the section on the "Master and Slave" dialectic, and that had a huge impact on me. This was when I was a research student. But I had already read Hegel's *Lectures on Aesthetics*, which were enormously influential because Hegel was the first modern philosopher to take art as seriously as it demands to be taken. He showed art to be both important and irreplaceable. For Hegel art is the sensuous embodiment of the Idea, the presentation in immediate experience of something that cannot be put into discursive terms.

'Hegel had an extraordinary synthetic mind which enabled him to see into the heart of whatever he was dealing with. Although he is over-systematic and tries to squeeze everything into the model of the dialectic – that's the annoying part of him – he would not have been able to do what he did if he did not have both a need for system and a profound instinct for truth. What he writes about art, especially about Dutch painting, was a revelation to me. Here was a philosopher who was taking art as a "moment of consciousness", a way in which human beings have understood the world and made it into an arena of action for themselves. He was giving a philosophical underpinning to the conviction that I had acquired all those years before from John Law. So I started reading the *Phenomenology of Spirit* with a sense of entering into a realm of revelation. But I still don't know that work as I know the works of Kant.'

Hegel, that great figure in whose shadow most contemporary European philosophy has been written, was not the type of thinker people would generally boast about reading at Cambridge. 'That is true,' says Scruton, 'but there was a new movement, including philosophers like Charles Taylor in Canada, who had started Hegelizing. There was enough interest around to make it seem perfectly sensible. My first book, *Art and Imagination*,[16] which is my thesis, doesn't have a great deal of Hegel in it; it is respectful towards him, but it doesn't say too much about him. Still, I had set myself the task of doing in the language of analytical philosophy what Hegel had done – which was to put art into the centre of philosophy and to say why it is significant.' I interject to ask who had examined Scruton's thesis. Had Elizabeth Anscombe read it? 'No, I don't think she ever read anything which she had not herself written! Bernard Williams was one of the examiners, as I recall.'

The light is fading and it is obvious that Roger has something serious on his mind. 'I really need to do something before it gets dark: would you mind if we went to buy two chickens?' And so we leave Hegel and go out in pursuit of replacements for a couple of chickens that were killed the previous night by a fox. Such is the course of Scruton's daily life: seamlessly moving from philosophy to poultry without so much as a pause.

2

Becoming a Philosopher

'I am a normal bourgeois person'

In *News from Somewhere*, Scruton writes that in 'the Wiltshire claylands farmers do everything they can to keep the soil at bay. They cover it with scalpings, concrete it over, or ram it full of hardcore. As soon as the winter comes, they turn their backs on the fields to struggle with the more manageable mud of the farmyard. Rain on concrete is a cleansing force, the sole natural ally in the war against the soil; rain on the fields is an adjunct of the enemy.'[1] As we drive to fetch the chickens, it is raining heavily on the Wiltshire claylands. Even though we are surrounded by the evening shadows, the beauty of this place is still apparent. Still, I now understand what Scruton meant when he wrote, also in *News from Somewhere*, that 'wet soil is belligerent, invasive, coating everything in a veneer of slime'. I look down at my feet only to find that they have fallen victim to this belligerent force. 'I have a pair of wellingtons which you will need to wear,' reflects Roger as he notices that familiar veneer on my shoes.

Our conversation brings us back to Cambridge and the philosophers that Scruton read during his studies. 'We would read someone like Quine, who is quite difficult, but we would also read all around him – all the commentaries – so as to try to get it right. There was a group of quite minor figures in the history of philosophy, who congregated in the middle of the twentieth century on both sides of the Atlantic – people like Carnap and the logical positivists – and we knew them quite well. The great thinkers, such as Aristotle, we had to discover for ourselves. Aristotle had never been incorporated into the syllabus. As one got to know him, of course, one came to see that he was doing exactly the same thing as Wittgenstein.'

I ask why it was that analytical philosophy seemed to have disowned Aristotle when, one could reasonably argue, he was its father? 'Here is the great difference between Cambridge and Oxford: Aristotle was not studied much in Cambridge and only a few people were doing Ancient philosophy. But in Oxford he was taken very seriously because of people like David Wiggins.' Wiggins was Wykeham Professor of Logic at Oxford from 1993 to 2000. He is the author of six highly influential books, most notably *Sameness and Substance*. A good friend of Scruton, he shall be visiting Sunday Hill Farm during my stay. For Wiggins, 'there is nobody who compares with Aristotle, and all analytic philosophy has been a prolonged effort at rediscovering what Aristotle clearly knew'.

Throughout his years at Cambridge, Scruton was continuously writing. 'I wrote,' he says, 'from the moment I had the calling to be a writer, which I got when I was sixteen. I didn't know how to do it, but I wrote every day and I always have done. Back then I wrote little stories and poems, which have mostly not survived. I wanted to write a few hundred words each day and wanted something to come out of it. I used to write letters to friends. Yes, I wrote all the time.' Anyone who has read Scruton will be struck by his prolific output. Yet when I ask him if, in those early years, he found writing easy, he responds quite categorically: 'No, I never did. I didn't find writing easy until I was in the middle of my life, around the age of thirty-five. I don't have a great talent and I'm not a natural, not the Rimbaud type. I get where I get by hard work. I decided to do it and I forced myself to do it and it has taken me a long time to acquire any ease with it. Nothing like a style of my own came until very late. I suppose journalism helped. Until trying my hand at journalism I had not really written anything that had satisfied me as a work of literature. I felt *Art and Imagination* was, intellectually, very respectable, but it is cluttered with technicalities and with analytical theories that are no longer relevant. I will say, however, that the theory of imagination I expound in that book still seems right to me, even if my writing style in it does not flow. It began to flow a bit more in *The Aesthetics of Architecture*, which I published in 1979.[2] That too has some clotted chapters, but here and there it has moments of proper writing.'

Having written so much in his spare time at Cambridge, did Scruton manage to get anything published? 'Only a little essay which appeared in an undergraduate magazine. I didn't really know how to publish.' So it wasn't like it is now when young academics must publish or perish? 'No it wasn't like that at all. Some of the people who taught us would have published things, but most of them published next to nothing. Or they might have one article on which they had worked for years. Casimir Lewy, who taught all of us logic, had just a few articles to his name.' Scruton's point about Lewy, who moved to the UK from Poland in 1936 and who died in Cambridge in 1991, is reinforced by Canadian philosopher Ian Hacking, who wrote of the logician: 'He had early acquired the conviction that one should publish only when one got something absolutely right, so he left very little in print.'

The philosopher who most impressed Scruton was, however, P. F. Strawson. From 1968 to 1987, Strawson was Waynflete Professor of Metaphysical Philosophy at Oxford, and author, in 1966, of the hugely influential *The Bounds of Sense: An Essay on Kant's Critique of Pure Reason.*[3] 'In that book, and in *Individuals: An Essay in Descriptive Metaphysics,*[4] he had a vision which made metaphysics "sound" again. We knew again what metaphysics was and that it could say something to us, even though its only message was that the common-sense world is OK. The book on Kant is a very elegant and eloquent account, but, in the end, it is too detached. It doesn't have the real sense that Kant gives you, that all these arguments concerning the limits of knowledge are won by hard work at the flaming edge of things – that place where the empirical gives out and the transcendental glimmers.'

In so many of Scruton's works we are brought to precisely this point where the empirical gives out and the transcendental glimmers. Was this something, contra Strawson, which he saw in Kant from the beginning? 'No, that came very much later. I actually took Jonathan Bennett's view of Kant as, essentially, a sceptical philosopher who showed the limits of human reason. I think that is definitely part of what Kant did: he showed that you cannot think beyond those limits. The cheap aspect of Hegel was that he believed you could both define the limits and also transcend them, so as to see the boundary from the other side. He didn't see the grandeur of what Kant had achieved.' I put it to Scruton that his philosophical vision has been shaped by Kant, but his worldview has been shaped by Hegel? 'Absolutely, yes, my political conceptions are very Hegelian. The first book of mine, when I actually began to write from the heart, was *The Meaning of Conservatism*, which was published in 1980. The book is a mess, but it was written from a heart that was very much inspired by Hegel.'[5]

We arrive at the chicken farmer's only to discover the place is vacant. The two surviving chickens will have to spend a second night alone at Sunday Hill Farm. Driving home, our discussion turns again to the British philosophical establishment. A. J. Ayer infamously said of Scruton's book *Sexual Desire* that it was 'silly'. 'I never met Ayer,' says Scruton, 'but he was part of a group of stuck-up Oxford dons who just *knew* that they were cleverer than everyone else, and who sneered at anyone who might be characterized as a conservative. I was regarded as fair game.' Elizabeth Anscombe, Scruton's doctoral director, and her husband Peter Geach, both of them orthodox Roman Catholics, did not belong to that set. 'However,' Scruton adds, 'they weren't just old-fashioned English eccentrics: they were bonkers! I mean as people, that is; not as philosophers, in which capacity they were among the last surviving manifestations of real common sense.'

What of the so-called continental philosophers, such as Sartre and Edmund Husserl: when did he begin reading them? Husserl would, in time, provide Scruton with his notion of the *Lebenswelt*, or the life-world, to which he has devoted much of his recent writing. 'I always read Nietzsche, and while at Cambridge I became very interested in Spinoza and Leibniz as well as Kant. I tried reading Heidegger at school, thanks to George Steiner's book *Martin Heidegger*, which I found unintelligible. I tried to read *Being and Time* and little bits did rub off, but none of it made much sense until I read those famous opening lines of 'Burnt Norton', Part One of T. S Eliot's *Four Quartets*:

> Time present and time past
> Are both perhaps present in time future
> And time future contained in time past.
> If all time is eternally present
> All time is unredeemable.

Suddenly, I realized you could think about time in a way which showed the beauty of it – the beauty of being *here and now*. That was something that struck me very vividly on reading Eliot, but it was not something I got from Heidegger.

'I suppose it is part of my analytical training that I don't admire philosophers for their wisdom, or their ability to give inspirational thoughts. I admire them because of their arguments, especially if they strike me as valid. I treat them more as scientific figures than as literary figures. But when there is a philosopher who is transparently a literary figure as well – such as Sartre, Schopenhauer or Nietzsche – then I feel a tremendous surge of approval. I feel this is what redeems philosophy, that it can translate itself into real literature. Sartre's *Being and Nothingness*, for example, is a masterpiece. To some extent, I feel about Sartre what I also feel about Rousseau, who was a great genius and a wonderful writer. Sartre was able to imbue the world with his own spirit and to make it look back at him in a confirming way. He said no to the world, and it looked back at him, saying yes to his no. I think Diderot was similar.

'Such people are real philosophers, but they are also people who make philosophy continuous with the life of the imagination. There was nothing affirmative in Sartre, but there was, nevertheless, the imaginative endeavour to present what life is like "to me, Jean-Paul Sartre". Diderot did that too, and he had a fantastic imagination, the greatest of any abstract thinker. Such is the kind of thinking you find in France since the Enlightenment, which perhaps doesn't count as *strictly* philosophical, but is nonetheless full of arguments and a conception of the fullness and the meaning of life. This is where literature and philosophy come together, where the concept and the image combine. Nietzsche was very aware of this, which is why he described his own writing as "musical", and pretended to be a Frenchman in a German body.'

To have enthusiastically embraced writers like Sartre, Nietzsche and Diderot, those in whom the concept and the image combine, profoundly distinguished Scruton from the philosophical milieu at Cambridge. Did this signal that his cultural side could not be suppressed in that analytical environment, but was always seeking a way to express itself? 'Oh yes, definitely. I have always been looking for the right way to say things, and for a way in which the peculiar subjectivity that is mine can find a voice that makes contact with others. I have wanted to give expression to my inner life, but have always been aware of the fact that the inner life is, to a great extent, a fiction. It is only there because you can give expression to it. And if you haven't managed to give expression to it, then it isn't there.'

It is dusk as we settle back into Scruton's study. I ask him if, during his time at university, he had any serious conservative convictions. 'After my first degree was completed in 1965, I went straight away to France, stopping in Paris on my way to Pau in the Pyrenees. I wasn't political then and things hadn't yet erupted over there as they would three years later. All that French Marxism was, however, very much in the air, and one was expected to be some kind of *gauchiste*. The people that I first met in Paris, I met through Anne Le Moal – whom I had known at Cambridge and who was the daughter of the famous painter Jean Le Moal. They were people associated with the theatre of playwright Armand Gatti. Gatti had, in turn, been greatly influenced by Antonin Artaud.'

Artaud, who had spent time in an Irish jail before being deported in 1937 as 'a destitute and undesirable alien', influenced a whole generation of people who were, as Scruton describes them, 'bohemian, leftist and wrapped up in psychoanalytic jargon'. He continues: 'I was then introduced to the writings of Michel Foucault, as the guru who was important for the people whom I was meeting. A year later, after my mother's death, I was in Italy where the Communist Party was very strong. There weren't only communists in local government: there was also a takeover of the schools by a Marxist cadre. That was very evident and the bourgeoisie had been marginalized and intimidated. The respectable Catholic Italy was hiding in the corner. That alerted me to what was going on and to the need to take sides. To my surprise, I found that my natural instinct was to take sides with the bourgeoisie.

'This was surprising because I was also a bohemian back then. When I was in Rome, I was again living hand-to-mouth, renting a room from a girl who rented a house in the Piazza del Biscione, just off the Campo dei Fiori. Her name was Elena Einaudi and her father was a big-cheese publisher, who was the familiar combination of Marxist and millionaire. She had fled from him and repudiated her parents, but remained in contact with her grandmother, widow of Italy's first post-war president. Sometimes we would visit old Signora Einaudi in the villa that had been provided for her outside the city walls. She would give us tea and cakes and look sadly at Elena's scruffy countenance while lamenting the times into which she had, without meaning to, survived. Elena identified herself as a lost bohemian soul who was making her own mark in life by belonging with the "victims". Although I too was a bohemian and surviving very much at the bottom of things, I was always quite repelled by her "victim" posture. Funnily enough, however, contact with Elena's bohemian, hippy circle in Rome did make me realize that whatever I am, I am not *that*. That was in 1966, the year of protests against the Vietnam War, when students in America were following the example set by Buddhist monks in Vietnam and burning themselves alive.

'There was an enterprise called the "Living Theatre", a sort of American travelling theatre that did little tableau which they would take from place to place like the Pagliacci. They were quite famous at the time. They would march up and down the stage reading all the numbers on a dollar bill and making Nazi salutes. This was by way of impressing on the audience the "real" meaning of the dollar! They had a certain talent, but it was mostly of that childish kind. Anyway, they came and dumped themselves on Elena in the place where I was staying. There was a room where they could all sleep on the floor, and there they would smoke cannabis and make slow, sage remarks about how it's all kind of creepy out there, know what I mean? I am grateful to them, for they helped me to discover that I am a normal bourgeois person.

'A couple of years later, after I had gone back to do research at Cambridge, Danielle, whom I had met during my year in Pau and who later became my wife, came to live with me. That didn't work out because she couldn't stand the Cambridge atmosphere, and I fully understood that. So she went back to France to teach in a school and I would go to visit her. This was coming up to May 1968, so I was in Paris on and off through all those events. But it was my experience in Italy that made me conscious of the difference between self-indulgent disorder and carefully maintained order. And, without knowing much about it, I was on the side of order.'

This, however, did nothing to change Scruton's bohemianism because, as he says, 'I had no money, no job, and I survived by giving English lessons. I couldn't be anything *but* a bohemian. But I didn't like those hippies – especially the American ones who had such a high opinion of themselves, the sole ground for which was that they were in a state of rebellion against their parents. You know, I had a father against whom it was quite legitimate to be in a state of rebellion, but I didn't go around announcing it to the world and making it into my way of life. Whereas they, mostly spoilt brats from middle-class households, thought this was a vindication of their existence and a proof of their creative genius.' It was also the case, I suggest, that such people had a good deal of philosophical backup for their rebellious way of life. 'Oh yes, that was the time of Norman O. Brown, Herbert Marcuse and all the campus frolics in California. And it was built around the drug culture. On the other hand, as we now see, that culture was totally empty and ephemeral.'

Scruton proceeds to say that he told Elena she should 'get rid' of her tenants. However, 'on the back of them came another guy called Doc Hughes, who had written a big novel in the Thomas Pynchon style. He was an intelligent man, but was obviously paranoid and came with the familiar story that the CIA was after him. He would look outside the window and say "Look, that's their car! I recognize that number plate!" Anyway, he latched on to Elena and she fell madly for him. I tried to get her away from him but it was no good. He made her pregnant and then disappeared, as such people do. She had the baby, but by then I had left for England and she was on her own, a very vulnerable creature who had made the mistake of wanting to harm no one, not even those who did her harm. She moved house and lived on her own with the baby, refusing help from her parents, who didn't want to have anything to do with her anyway. In any case, the baby fell ill with German measles. Elena caught it from the baby and suffered alone and neglected in a little cupboard off the Via Giulia. She was discovered dead after three days with the baby still alive. They saved the baby, who is now in his late forties. He has told his story and has become quite a figure. I didn't know about Elena's death until later. I couldn't have done anything about it, since Doc stood like an armed sentry between her and the world, until he had fixed her fate and then left her to it. But I blamed myself too.'

As I would discover throughout our conversations, this man whom I thought I knew so well had experienced moments of great poignancy in the course of his unusual life. As the night closes in, and as he lights the lamps in a study that was made for candlelight, I take him back to 1971, when he got his first real job as a lecturer in the Department of Philosophy at Birkbeck College in London.

3

Becoming a Conservative at Birkbeck

'I was a rebel against rebellion'

From 1971 to 1991, Scruton taught at Birkbeck, first as lecturer and subsequently as Reader and Professor of Aesthetics in the Philosophy Department. It was during this time that he 'came out' as a conservative in the mould of Edmund Burke. It was also the period in which he rose to prominence as a public figure whose views were often regarded as purposefully controversial. I begin by asking him how he got the job at Birkbeck. 'In 1967, I went back to Cambridge to do research at Jesus College. I put in for a Research Fellowship at Peterhouse during the course of my next year. In fact, I was offered a fellowship at two other colleges also, I don't know why. My dissertation probably got sent to the same person by each of them, and that person didn't see that it was just pretentious gibberish.

'Anyway, I decided to go to Peterhouse, partly because of its conservative reputation. After coming back to Cambridge with the burden of my experience in Italy and France, I was looking for a way to articulate my disapproval of the way things were going, and to find an alternative to the culture of youth and the politics of rebellion. To me the Sixties were redolent of The Living Theatre and Doc Hughes's self-centred fight against an imaginary "system". I was a rebel against rebellion without knowing exactly what to put in its place. However, I met John Casey and the Peterhouse historian Maurice

Cowling, who gave me the sense that it was really quite reasonable to swim against the tide, and that they themselves had a philosophy with which to justify doing so.

'At Peterhouse, there was a school of conservative historians – Edward Norman, Cowling, Roger Lovatt, Brian Wormald – and a general atmosphere of slightly "Max Beerbohmish" rejection of the proletarian culture. I found this quite exciting at first, though I intensely disliked the pederastic atmosphere of Cambridge, and always wondered why it was necessary, in order to affect the heights of sophistication, to be so entirely camp. I remained convinced that you could be an apostle of high culture and also heterosexual, though I appreciated that this heretical position ought not to be blatantly displayed to those who might be offended by it.

'By then, I was taking my career very seriously and it was obvious that I was on the way back into the academy, even though an academic was something I hadn't thought of being. Even if it was to be my career, however, it was a very precarious one: by then the new universities had filled all their posts, and there was next to nothing available. But then a lectureship came up in Birkbeck College, London. To my surprise I got the job, and was able to move to London.

'Crucial to my life at the time was the fact that George Gale became editor of *The Spectator* magazine. He was a famous journalist of the old-fashioned, rude rightist kind, who was also a close friend of Maurice Cowling. Indeed, they lived in a *ménage à trois* with George Gale's wife Patricia. Patricia sought to lead a grand lifestyle in Wivenhoe, Essex, surrounded by exotic creatures from public life – people like Peregrine Worsthorne from the world of journalism and the more dazzling sort of politicians like Tony Crosland. Both Labour and Conservative politicians would gather at the Gales' house, though the core of their circle was a group of conservative intellectuals, including Kingsley Amis, Henry Fairlie and Paul Johnson.

'When George became editor of *The Spectator* he appointed Maurice as Literary Editor. That was my literary break. It was the first time I was asked to write something rather than begging unsuccessfully to have something published. My first published work was therefore a review of Terry Eagleton in *The Spectator*. I did a few more such reviews and George and Maurice liked them. I gradually acquired a way of articulating, in a slightly journalistic way, some of the things that were going on in my mind.

'In coming to London, therefore, I already had a circle of people with whom I was in contact – that is to say, the people around *The Spectator*. Arriving in London I had the good fortune to meet Delia Smith, the now famous cookery writer, at a *Spectator* party, who said that she was moving out of her flat and if I wanted to take it over she would recommend me. The flat was in a house in Harley Street, which belonged to Cicely Yudkin, from a quite famous Jewish family, and she took me on. Danielle came back from France to live with me there. She spent a year studying for the Graduate Certificate in Education, which she hated, in order to get a job. The rubbish that Danielle was required to study in the name of pedagogy awoke me for the first time to the calamity inflicted on our education system by the educationists, whose brain-deadening curriculum seemed designed to ensure that no real knowledge but only muddled ideology would enter the classroom. Still, Danielle struggled through the course, and took a job teaching French in Putney High School. We lived together for a while in London, though without really settling down.

'When I arrived at Birkbeck, my very first impression was that my colleagues had made a terrible mistake in choosing me and were already regretting what they had done. There was a pronounced hostility in the air. When I had applied for the job, I learned, they had approached Bernard Williams for a reference. He had, in effect, said: "This guy is good at the subject, but he's a repulsive conservative." So I didn't feel very welcome among people who had never met a conservative before, and who peered at me round the door of my office in order to ascertain whether I was doing the strange things that conservatives do, like boiling babies in test-tubes or marching up and down making Nazi salutes.

'David Hamlyn was Professor of Philosophy at the time. He was a very honourable and hardworking man who had built up the department as one of the strongest in London. He was someone with a Baptist upbringing, a very correct person – shy but definite in everything, and somewhat lacking in humour. Ruby Meager was also there and her subject was aesthetics. It was very useful for me to have someone interested in my subject, and at first

I had big plans to make a speciality of aesthetics. But I wasn't specifically hired to do that, and soon found that I was teaching ethics and the history of philosophy instead. There was a syllabus to cover and the topics were distributed fairly arbitrarily.

'You have to remember that the events of Paris, May 1968, were just hitting London in 1971. There was a delayed reaction, since it takes time for a new idea to enter an English head. I made my views about May 1968 pretty clear. Our classes took place in the evenings and we weren't allowed to lecture before six o'clock, because the Birkbeck students were in full-time employment. Although not necessarily young firebrands, they were nonetheless moving in a radical direction. They were very serious and I learned so much from them. They were, however, on the left and people on the left think that *everything* is political. Even if you are discussing the foundations of arithmetic they will look for the hidden political agenda. Every question and every answer, when you are fully immersed in the left-wing way of thinking, is part of a political posture. Indeed, to suppose that there are purely impartial and objective questions is itself to be guilty of "right-wing" deviationism. Against that way of arguing you cannot possibly win, and that, I came to realize, is its point – just as you cannot win an argument about the Qur'an with someone who recognizes no authority other than the Qur'an.

'So, no, I didn't do very well in persuading people that I was an acceptable member of the community. But I stuck it out. I found my circle of friends and companions outside the university. I became very friendly with the *Spectator* crowd and journalists like Peter Utley. And I also got to know the writer Antonia Fraser, who greatly impressed me with her style and her knowledge of the world and, through her husband, Hugh Fraser, I began to become acquainted with a few Conservative politicians. Despite my shyness I acquired a widening circle of friends beyond the university.'

And what of Scruton's publishing career during these early days at Birkbeck? 'I was publishing a bit but it hadn't really taken off. I did publish my thesis *Art and Imagination: A Study in the Philosophy of Mind* with Methuen in 1974. That was my first major publication. But by the time of *Art and Imagination*, I had decided that maybe I shouldn't be part of a university anyway. I couldn't find there the life that I really wanted, which would be both a life of the mind and a conservative public posture. Because I was teaching in the evenings, I had my days free and could do a full-time course of study. So I started reading for the Bar in 1974 and was called in 1978. I did the crash course, where you could pass all three exams in two years. I never regretted doing that, but unfortunately I couldn't afford to take pupillage – which then meant a year of unpaid apprenticeship – and thus I never practised.'

What Scruton failed to mention was that he won both the Struben and Profumo prizes in reading for the Bar in 1975. His studies also gave him a deep appreciation for the law, especially the English common law about which he has written so often and so convincingly. For example, in his moving tribute to the country of his birth, *England: An Elegy*, Scruton responds to those who protest that 'the law is a human artefact, that it exists only because we are disposed to regulate our lives in legal terms, and that it has no "independent reality"'. The Cathedral of St Paul's is, he argues, 'a human artefact: does that imply that it has no "independent reality"? Look again at the reasoning of the courts: it is not a process of "invention", but a process of discovery. And even if, in some broad sense, the legal system is a work of the human imagination, this is at best a proof that the imagination is sometimes needed if the world is to be seen as it is. The English law was an attempt to understand the human world; it both uncovered and endorsed the impartial justice whereby the English people ordered their lives. And by measuring the world against an ideal it showed the world as it is.'[1] Such sentiments run right through all Scruton's writings on conservatism and reflect, as he puts it to me, 'the strong love that I developed for the English common law and the wonderful concepts that come out of it – such as the concepts of equity, trust and occupier's liability'.

Not being in a position to practise law, Scruton continued to move in 'circles outside the university. I got to know John Gross, who was appointed editor of the *Times Literary Supplement* in 1974, a position he held until 1981. In my view, he was the most enlightened editor the *TLS* ever had, and he saw this as an opportunity to put down a marker for the kind of worldview that he espoused. He invited liberal-conservative thinkers, pariahs like me, to write reviews, and he took seriously the question of developing an argument and a philosophy through the journal, just as Sartre had done, to opposite effect, in *Les temps modernes*. In fact, I had written a review of Gross's book on James Joyce, published in the Fontana Modern Masters series in 1971. That was reprinted in *The Politics of Culture and Other Essays*, which came out in 1981.[2] It was a terrific inspiration for me to get my thoughts on Joyce into one article. Thanks to John, more of those things came my way. I also became good friends with Michael Schmidt, who was General Editor of *PN Review*, which he helped to found in 1973. I began writing a few things for him as well.'

With his writing career beginning to take off, did this heighten the antipathy towards Scruton at Birkbeck? 'The academic world is full of back-biting, but Birkbeck was traditionally a left-wing place, haunted by the fear that somewhere, somehow, a conservative might have infiltrated the corridors. Eric Hobsbawm was resident guru and, as far as I could see, the Master was always appointed by Transport House. It really wasn't the place for me, but the students were terrific because they were all grown up.' I interrupt to ask who were his most famous students. 'The most famous students I had were actually from a batch of graduates I taught at King's College, Cambridge, when I was just one year ahead of them – David Papineau, who is Professor of Philosophy at King's now, and Jonathan Sacks – now Lord Sacks – who became Chief Rabbi. Ian McFetridge was actually the cleverest of them, and he became a lecturer at Birkbeck and a close friend. Unfortunately he had bipolar disorder and killed himself while in a deep depression – a great blow to me, since he validated my life as a teacher more than any student I have had. Anyway, by 1979 I was really moving outside the university circle altogether.'

At the end of the 1970s, Scruton set about writing his first major statement on conservative thought. *The Meaning of Conservatism* was published in 1980, thus making its author the *bête noire* for those of opposing political views. And it is easy to see why, for in the 'Introduction' to this work he writes:

Conservatives, who see value in prejudice and danger in abstract thought, have extemporised, expressing their beliefs in vague and conciliatory language. However, neither the socialist nor the liberal can be appeased. Their bigotry (and there is no greater bigotry, I shall suggest, than the bigotry of liberalism) permits no conciliation, while their statements seem clear, definite, founded in a system. Until conservatives lay hold again of the principles which motivate them, they will find themselves outwitted by those who lay claim to a conviction which they may not always feel but are always ready to express.[3]

Such views were formed in the course of a long apprenticeship observing the vanguard of what Scruton calls 'the culture of repudiation'. He witnessed their antics on the streets of Paris in 1968, in Elena Einaudi's house in Rome and at Birkbeck College, which 'contained, to my knowledge, two conservatives: myself, and Nunzia (Annunziata), the Neapolitan lady who served behind the counter in the Senior Common Room, and who showed her contempt for the fellow travellers who queued there by plastering her patch of wall with photographs of the Pope. Nunzia was the only person I could really talk to in the university, and it is not surprising, therefore, if this book [*The Meaning of Conservatism*] – my first attempt to write about politics – did not conform to the accepted standards of academic politeness.'[4]

But how did this first great tract on his political worldview come about? 'The philosopher Ted Honderich was appointed by Penguin Books to produce philosophical books on the various political positions. He needed one on conservatism and I was the only philosophical conservative that he knew. So he asked me to do it. It was an improvised book because I am not a political scientist. I put it together out of my sparse reading and my abundant sentiments! It was provocative and, of course, created a stir. Inside Birkbeck, the reception was *very* hostile, but I didn't know the people sufficiently to worry about it. I was not addressing my leftist colleagues but the people who had supported Mrs Thatcher [who had come to power in 1979] – the free marketeers and their libertarian ideologues. And I was trying to say that conservatism is something *other* than what they believed it to be.

'After its publication, the Marxist philosopher at University College London, Jerry (G. A.) Cohen, refused to teach a seminar with me. Jerry was brought up as a believing communist in a little circle of the same in Montreal. He couldn't cope with what he saw as a sin, as well as a huge provocation. Later though, Jerry, whom I very much admired, moved in a conservative direction, and responded very warmly to my books on architecture and hunting. I was deeply upset by his sudden death in 2009, just at the moment when we were becoming friends again. In 1980, however, ideas like mine were simply unheard of in the universities and Jerry in particular found them deeply offensive. In the library at Birkbeck you couldn't find, in the politics section, a book by any living conservative thinker – not even by Michael Oakeshott or Friedrich Hayek. There was a real sense that the conservative position is evil, and that sense is still there in the academic world. Just yesterday, I was in London for a panel discussion on the Human Rights Act with the Professor of Law from Birkbeck. And I encountered the same old snide response, laughing contemptuously whenever the word "conservative" is mentioned.

'At the same time, I published *The Politics of Culture and Other Essays* (1981) and also my first novel, *Fortnight's Anger*,[5] which I had written over many years. That novel was an attempt to come to terms with all kinds of troubling things that I had not been able to digest. It is a total failure as a novel because it has no drama in it and is far too introspective. Still, I wasn't intending to publish it. I sent it to Michael Schmidt simply for his opinion and he put it on his list at Carcanet Press without asking my permission until it was in the press!'

By 1982, Scruton was out of the closet as a conservative and was a marked man. Things only got worse, however, because of his involvement with the Salisbury Group, named after Robert Gascoyne-Cecil, 3rd Marquess of Salisbury and former British Prime Minister. He explains: 'In 1981, the Salisbury Group wanted to set up a *Review* of intellectual conservatism and they asked me to be the editor of the *Review*, the first edition of which came out in 1982. I didn't know many conservative politicians, though Hugh

Fraser and Jonathan Aitken had become friends through the Conservative Philosophy Group, which we had collaborated in founding, together with John Casey, in 1974. Through the Salisbury Group, however, I did get to know many conservative journalists. They were a weird collection of people, some of whom were useless old cranks and some of whom were very interesting. Maurice Cowling was part of it. Today there are younger conservative MPs who are interested in what I have to say. But back then I had no standing in the Conservative Party or among conservative politicians. To them, I was just a weird intellectual sounding off. Hence, getting *The Salisbury Review* going was incredibly hard. I had to find people who could express serious conservative thoughts, and who could put them together in an article. I really enjoyed it but it was also a great effort putting together a magazine, most of which, in the beginning, I had to write myself under various pseudonyms. I had to make it look as though there was something there in order that *there should be something there*! I am sure all small magazines begin in that way.'

This was, however, the early period of the Thatcher era, one in which Britain would finally be released from its socialist yoke. Was Scruton impressed with her at first? 'Not really. Of course, I was very glad she was there because she changed the atmosphere completely. Overnight, all the people around me in the university had acquired something to hate! It all became clear in their minds, just as it became equally clear in mine. One of the things that history tells us is that, when there is strong leadership, it takes only a day and a night for a country to wake up, as France did under Napoleon and Poland under Wałęsa. It was difficult for Mrs Thatcher at first because she didn't have the complex ideological perspective that would have enabled her to speak to the intellectuals. But she did have clear ideas that she could broadcast to the ordinary people.'

Was Scruton proud of his country under Thatcher? 'I've always been proud of my country, actually: not necessarily for what it is but for what it *was*.' But surely she brought back something of what it was? 'Oh yes, of course she did. She was very lucky with the Falklands War because something of the old spirit of Empire immediately came into play. And, indeed, the people were totally behind her. I meet a lot of young people who long to find again that thread of connection with the English idea, and who would, in a crisis, stand up, as people did then.'

In the midst of the heat that surrounded *The Meaning of Conservatism*, Scruton was proving himself to be a publishing sensation. Following publication of *The Politics of Culture* and *Fortnight's Anger* in 1981, there appeared *A Short History of Modern Philosophy: From Descartes to Wittgenstein* and, in 1982, *The Dictionary of Political Thought*, a book that is now in its third edition and one that runs to nearly eight hundred pages.[6] Also in 1982, Scruton published his monograph *Kant: A Short Introduction*, which is still regarded as one of the finest introductions to that thinker in print.[7] I ask Scruton if such serious and prodigious writing frustrated those, in the academy and beyond, who would have otherwise cast him off as an ideological charlatan? 'Obviously, it was annoying that I was capable of serious academic work. Unfortunately, however, my interests were primarily in those areas of philosophy that deal with culture: not just art, but also the places where the human world demands examination. That sort of thing does not have a recognized place in analytical philosophy. And so, people would feel able to dismiss my work as *merely* ideological, because the non-ideological side they would regard as marginal and uninteresting, or else as a cryptic expression of conservative views. None of my philosophical colleagues saw, for example, the relevance to intellectual life of what I was trying to do in *The Aesthetics of Architecture*. Of course, there were those in aesthetics who took an interest in the book. Indeed, it has been, in many ways, one of my most influential works because, for all its faults, it helped to define the subject. My book on Kant is not scholarship, but an attempt to present Kant as clearly as I can. It is true that many have found it useful. I think Kant would have found it useful! I wrote that book very quickly in Prague – in four days actually. The whole thing just became totally clear to me. I had worked and worked on Kant and I had given a course of lectures on him several times at London University. Those lectures were actually quite well known because people had recorded them.'

Scruton explains that 'people on the left don't, on the whole, engage with their opponents. They dismiss and sneer at them, and, if they can, they will accuse them of things like racism or whatever the evil of the day might be (today it is homophobia, though I see *transphobia* looming over the horizon too). So I obviously got all that, but I don't get it so much now.'

Before travelling to Wiltshire for our conversations, I read the manuscript of the revised and updated version of Scruton's most notorious book, *Thinkers of the New Left*, which was first published in 1985. Now titled *Fools, Frauds and Firebrands: Thinkers of the New Left*, it is a book that I had been encouraging Scruton to reissue for some years.[8] This was because it not only provides a devastating critique of those who have served as high priests to the new left, but also contains some of the most powerful analysis of those ideas which have gripped the intellectual world since the 1960s. In the original, Scruton was uncompromising:

> The message of the New Left was simple. All power in the world is oppressive, and all power is usurped. Abolish that power and we achieve justice and liberation together. The new generation was not disposed to ask the fundamental question; the question of how social justice (understood according to some egalitarian paradigm) might be reconciled with liberation. It wished only for the authoritative assurance that would validate its parricide, and received that assurance from the dirge-like incantations of the left. The new thinkers turned attention away from the difficult task of describing the socialist future to the easy holiday of destruction. They made fury respectable, and gobbledegook the mark of academic success. With the hasty expansion of the universities and polytechnics, and the massive recruitment of teachers from the over-fished and under-nourished generation, the status of the New Left was assured. Suddenly whole institutions of learning were in the hands of people who had identified the rewards of intellectual life through fantasies of collective action, and who had seen the principal use of theory in its ability to smother the questions that would provide too sturdy an impediment to *praxis*. For such people the New Left was the paradigm of successful intellectual endeavour.[9]

Looking back, it is easy to see why such statements made Scruton the bogeyman of the left establishment. However, his essays on Michel Foucault, Antonio Gramsci, Louis Althusser, György Lukács and Jean-Paul Sartre demonstrate a powerfully intuitive grasp of these thinkers' intellectual shortcomings. Also, the fact that this book earned Scruton so much calumny in no way detracts from the truth of its claims. In the introduction to the new edition, *Fools, Frauds and Firebrands*, Scruton glances back to the firestorm generated by the original:

> My previous book was published at the height of Margaret Thatcher's reign of terror, at a time when I was still teaching in a university, and known among British left-wing intellectuals as a prominent opponent of their cause, which was the cause of decent people everywhere. The book was therefore greeted with derision and outrage, reviewers falling over each other for the chance to spit on the corpse. Its publication was the beginning of the end for my university career, the reviewers raising serious doubts about my intellectual competence as well as my moral character. This sudden loss of status led to attacks on all my writings, whether or not they touched on politics.[10]

I ask Scruton how these doubts regarding his intellectual competence and moral character affected him personally. 'It was a disaster. I did actually feel somewhat suicidal after that because I put much more work into that book than people thought. It is, I believe, quite well written and encapsulates a distinctive vision. It is also respectful towards most of its targets. So it was a perfectly legitimate work in my view, but it was dismissed out of hand and with incredible malice.'

On 4 January 1983, Roger Scruton penned his first column for *The Times* newspaper. He would feature on an almost weekly basis until August 1986. His inaugural column was on the subject of education and it articulated ideas that still exercise Scruton. Entitled 'The Virtue of Irrelevance', this article set out Scruton's stall in typically strident, yet no less colourful tones: 'This is the secret which civilisation has guarded: that power and influence come through the acquisition of useless knowledge. The answer is, therefore, to destroy the effect of education by making it relevant. Replace pure by applied mathematics, logic by computer programming, architecture by engineering, history by sociology: the result will be a new generation of well-informed philistines, whose charmlessness will undo every advantage which their learning might otherwise have conferred.'

Later on, he writes that

[c]onsiderable ingenuity has been spent in inventing 'relevant' humanities. The problem has been to conserve the outward prestige of education, as an embodiment of the reasonable approach to life's problems, while persuading the uneducated that there is a learning addressed to interests which they already have. The answer has been found in the word 'studies'. When added to a relevant-sounding prefix (such as 'media' or 'communications', 'black' or 'gay') this word adjoins even to the most half-baked enthusiasm an air of superior knowledge.[11]

From this alone, it is easy to see why Sir Peter Stothard, the then features editor at *The Times*, subsequently wrote that 'there was no one I ever commissioned to write whose articles provoked more rage'.[12]

Scruton tells me how he came to write *The Times* column: 'I had been in touch with Peter Stothard because he was interested in *The Salisbury Review*. He had also come along to a Conservative Philosophy Group meeting and naughtily written about it when he shouldn't have done, which caused a slight problem! But he thought it would be great to give me a try. So he asked me to do a weekly column. As someone like you will know, this is a great privilege. I did it for four years, at a time when Mrs Thatcher was at her height. Hatred of the Conservative Party and the Prime Minister was uniform in the academic world, and it was regarded as an act of betrayal for a university teacher to be writing a regular column supporting her. In particular, I did two things that really upset people: I took on the anti-racist nonsense and made fun of it, and also I took on the Peace Movement. Those two issues were the real heart of leftist thinking in our universities. I was also taking a stance against Soviet strategy, of which the fellow travellers were not necessarily a conscious part, although they were linked to people like Hobsbawm and Ralph Miliband who were then consciously on the Soviet side.'

One column, from January 1984, illustrates the approach that Scruton took to ensure his demonization among the so-called 'peace' activists of the academic world. Peace studies, he wrote, is

> concerned to beg the only question that it could conceivably answer: the question of how peace is secured. I happen to believe that there is no way to preserve peace in Europe without matching the armaments, and blocking the expansionist policies, of the Soviet Union. That belief of mine is based on reasoning, the major premise of which is the nature and history of the Soviet Union. Take away the premise, and I should certainly arrive at a different conclusion. I may be wrong; but I know that any person who sets out to discuss this question without first considering the major premise is irrational, and that a subject which is devoted (as "peace studies" is devoted) to preventing all consideration of its own major premise is not an academic discipline but an exercise in propaganda.[13]

I point out, however, that Scruton's *Times* column was not only concerned with goading the left, but also included wonderful pieces on music, wine, fish, liturgical reform and motorcycle maintenance. 'Funny you should say that. Just last week, some ordinary person from America who had come across the column on repairing the motorbike, wrote to me to say how much he enjoyed it.' And when I recall that there were also some superb philosophical pieces on architecture, sex and the soul, Scruton responds that 'all that made it even more offensive because it made me look human! It needed that much more work to make me look like a monster. But there's no doubt that it was a difficult time for me. When, for example, it was time for me to be promoted to professor, the external referee wrote to the head of my department saying that he might have recommended me until I started writing those articles in *The Times*. But those articles had revealed my real intellectual capacities.

'I had the same opposition from within the university. But this, you see, is where you have to respect the left intellectuals: they don't think that because you are of the wrong ideology they are therefore justified in opposing you. They think that the ideology is proof of your stupidity. Like John Stuart Mill, they regard conservatives as "the stupider party". Therefore, they have a duty to oppose you, and they feel very sad about it. They push you aside with gestures of compassion. They would love to have helped you in your career, but their integrity as public-spirited professionals causes them reluctantly to oppose your promotion. After a while, like Winston in Orwell's *1984*, you begin to half believe their view of you. For a long time during the 1980s and 1990s I was unsure whether I had any real intellectual contribution to make, and half accepted the official view of myself as a marginal figure. I am more confident now, but it's still a question of whether I have the right to count myself on the same level as people like David Wiggins. Nothing has helped me recover my self-confidence more than the fact that David treats me as an intellectual equal, as Jerry Cohen also did. Though I should add that both of them have written works that I cannot hope to emulate.'

Scruton's columns were eventually collected in the book *Untimely Tracts*, which was published in 1987. Reading them now, it is remarkable how prescient so many of them were. Most of what he wrote regarding education, integration and conservative politics is now widely accepted as the truth. His robust stance against those who sought to appease the Soviet empire was justified by subsequent history. In light of this, I ask him if he now feels vindicated by the stance he took in those columns. 'I do think that the real cause of the hatred of me is that I said things which are true but which were then untimely. I actually wanted to call the book "Tracts for *The Times*", but *The Times* wouldn't allow me. So yes, I do feel somewhat vindicated. And it was, of course, useful money, although I was not totally unhappy when the column stopped.'

Before leaving our discussion of his stint on *The Times*, I ask Scruton about what was undoubtedly the most controversial moment of that period: the Honeyford Affair. In his column of 24 April 1984, Scruton outlined the specifics of what would become one of the darkest episodes of his career. He wrote:

> In the winter issue of *The Salisbury Review* an article appeared challenging the fashionable pieties concerning 'multi-cultural education'. Its author was Ray Honeyford, whose experience and education make it impossible for him to believe the nonsense put out by the Commission for Racial Equality (a government quango which survives by discovering racial conflicts where no one had previously noticed them). Mr Honeyford is a headmaster of a multi-racial school in Bradford. He must confront each day the fate of white working-class children, who constitute the 'ethnic minority' in a growing number of inner-city schools and whose educational opportunities are increasingly threatened ... He is brought into contact with the extensive propaganda against our schools and curriculum produced by people who despise our traditions of understatement, civilised discourse and respect for truth. He must deal with teachers who perceive the professional advantage of supporting multi-cultural education and of making race into the kind of 'high profile' issue that the sowers of discord would like it to be ... Mr Honeyford, with the natural instinct of the rational animal, recorded some of these experiences, drew attention to the problems presented by multi-cultural education, criticised the fatuity of fashionable solutions and presented, in British fashion, a sceptical conclusion. All of which is part of the normal operation of the spirit of compromise. Mr Honeyford's article came, however, to the attention of the local National Union of Teachers, which saw an opportunity to display that concern for truth and evidence which has ever been the virtue of the teaching profession. It passed the following resolution, and broadcast it to the world in a 'Press Statement':
>
> "We strongly condemn the views expressed by Ray Honeyford in an article in *The Salisbury Review*, winter 1984. We feel that these views contravene the local authority policies on race relations

and multicultural education. In the light of this, we urge the local authority to take immediate action and remove Mr Honeyford from his present post."

Mr Honeyford's article discusses critically the local authority's policies; therefore he contravened them, therefore he should be sacked. This totalitarian argument is clearly of wide application.

Scruton concluded his column with a denunciation of those who sought to terminate Ray Honeyford's teaching career, and succeeded in doing so: 'Mr Honeyford's crime was to tell the truth as he saw it. In particular, he told the truth about Pakistani politics – something that the left will allow when justifying Soviet policy, but not when praising British institutions. For this truth he must be silenced. The ruthless bigotry of those who wish to silence him is matched by their contempt for education. For such people, the dismissal of a headmaster of proven ability is a small price to pay for his replacement by one who spouts the same ignorant rubbish as themselves.'[14]

Scruton recalls that the Honeyford case 'caused me to be branded as a racist, and it meant that whenever I went to give public speeches in a university or anywhere, I had to confront a rent-a-mob who could be very threatening. I actually had to have police protection in York. I often wondered whether the whole thing was worth it, but having started on this track I felt that, well, if I don't do it, who is going to do it? I managed to get some friends and we worked on it together. Caroline Cox – now Baroness Cox – and John Marks, for example, both of whom had fought the very same battle at North London Polytechnic. So they came to my help and we, along with Jessica Douglas-Home and others, were determined to make this and similar issues prominent. With regard to the Honeyford case, it is now all water under the bridge and everybody recognizes that Ray was right. In fact, I was asked to write his entry for the *Dictionary of National Biography*. For me it was a vindication, and even the editors thought, yes, what I wrote was both true and an indictment of those who had subjected Ray to such persecution.'

4

Some Thoughts on British Philosophy

'My questions are almost never addressed'

We are in Roger Scruton's kitchen where he is preparing an evening meal of duck and egg salad. It is clear that 'Scrutopia', as he likes to call his world, is a place of food: food for thought, food for the soul and food from the farm. The eggs were collected that morning from the two surviving chickens, and the Bordeaux I have just sampled was taken from Roger's cellar, which is also located in the farmyard. 'As long as you have 365 bottles in stock, everything will be fine,' he tells me.

As he fries up some home-grown vegetables for a ratatouille, our conversation turns to the current state of British philosophy: 'I would love it to be a vital thing, an intellectual movement in which people are writing things that we all want to read – a community in full and open discussion. But I don't think it is like that now. It is true that there is much clever philosophy being written, but the analytical narrowness has driven away the human questions. That I find very depressing. The fact that the Oxford philosopher Derek Parfit is referred to as the greatest moral philosopher of our time is a sign of how isolated analytical philosophy has become. His utilitarian arguments are very clever, but there are no human beings in them! In answer to the question, 'how should I live?' he has nothing to say, or nothing that a grown person would not laugh at.

'There is a range of questions, in epistemology, semantics and philosophy of science, which everybody addresses, but my questions are almost never addressed, even though they are of the first importance. Only yesterday I was speaking to Simon May, who is a professor at King's College London. He has written a lovely book on love[1] and is currently writing a sequel. That first book is widely read and is also philosophically very competent, but he feels the same as I do, seeing himself as someone on the margins, who has lost contact with his discipline because it has lost contact with him.'

I ask Scruton whom he admires within the British philosophical establishment. 'I do admire David Wiggins and his writings on metaphysics, although they are technical and not an easy read. I also admire his book on ethics, which is so much more important than that by Derek Parfit, since it attempts to show how rational beings, living in communities, move of their own accord towards a conception of just dealings. Simon Blackburn's moral philosophy is also intriguing and tenaciously worked out. He's a bit more like me: he works hard on finding the right words to put across serious ideas. Simon and I were contemporaries at Cambridge and we know each other well.

'The generation before my own was abundantly supplied with intelligent and argumentative intellects. Austin, Strawson and Ryle deserve great praise for their attempt to put philosophy in the context of our everyday language and the metaphysical implications contained in it. Bernard Williams was also a very eloquent philosopher, although very bigoted, and influential partly because of that. He masked his bigotry with his sophisticated approach to everything, his sense of himself as looking down from a great height on the mistakes of mere mortals. Among those mere mortals I think there are very few to beat Thomas Nagel for elegance and for the application of philosophy to life in our shared world. But Tom is not British. The most important British philosopher of Williams's generation – Elizabeth Anscombe – was someone whom he despised on account of her Catholic faith, even though it is precisely her faith which now draws people to study her deep thoughts on intention and the philosophy of self-consciousness.

'Analytical philosophy began as an adversarial discipline – a self-sustaining dialogue of arguments, which had little or no interest in the real human world. Suddenly, in a moment of doubt around 1968, philosophers began to ask themselves what the point of it all was. There then arose a hundred versions of "applied philosophy", all in their own way as empty as Parfit's "moral arithmetic". Philosophy fragmented into specialisms – often defined by an ideological agenda. There is now an academic branch called "feminist philosophy". Do you imagine that it contains any members who are not feminists? Likewise there is a branch devoted to animal rights, with which I have had something to do, on account of having written a book arguing that there are no such things. Environmental ethics, queer philosophy, gender philosophy – all such branches of the subject have become theological, built around a foregone conclusion as theology is built around the existence of God. My book on *Green Philosophy* was an attempt to break into a protected domain, to start from philosophical first principles as I had done in *The Aesthetics of Architecture* and *The Aesthetics of Music* – and so far it has elicited no response that I am aware of from the many researchers in the field of environmental ethics, for the simple reason that its conclusions emerge at the end of its argument, and are not buried in the beginning.

'Analytical philosophy is clever. But it is also blind – blind to what matters in human experience, and blind to the realms of culture, art and religion. Hence it is easy to learn, and easy to apply. But it so readily destroys the thing to which it is applied, by rewriting it in terms of some favoured conclusion. Thus the feminist philosophers begin from their conclusion – that men and women are in all relevant respects the same, and that any disparities are to be explained in terms of the centuries of oppression exercised by the unfair sex. There is no arguing with the conclusion because it has been assumed all along, and long before it was stated. The result can hardly be called philosophy, and should really be relegated to the old category of "dogmatics", of which there are many dusty volumes in the theology sections of our libraries that have not been opened for years.

'It should be said, however, that this new kind of "relevant" philosophy – which is not relevant at all since it merely assumes what it should be disputing, and therefore leaves everything exactly as it was – is in part an attempt to bring philosophy into the centre of the intellectual life, in the way that it has always been on the continent.'

I ask Scruton to explain what he means. After a moment's thought he responds: 'This is something I used to think about a lot, in the days when I asked myself why it is that British philosophy, which has so much going for it, has lost ground to French and German philosophy in the battle of ideas. Why do we, who have devoted so much effort to developing the art of valid argument, seem to have so little use for it? I wrote something about this once, but it was never published.' I ask him to show me what he wrote, and I quote it here because it echoes sentiments that I have had myself, ever since acknowledging the great chasm that exists between so many continental philosophers, who once seemed so important to me, and Scruton, whose directness and scepticism have a special appeal of their own:

When I read philosophy in Cambridge in the sixties, the subject was called 'moral science', as it had been since it first was taught in that university. The prevailing view was that the term 'philosophy' had a pretentious and continental air, and would mislead students into believing that they would learn about the meaning of life. The word 'moral' was taken very seriously, nevertheless. There was not one but two compulsory papers on ethics in the first part of the tripos, even though metaphysics, logic and the philosophy of science had only one paper each. Students were required to read no historical figures, besides the masters of philosophical ethics, and their only acquaintance with German philosophy was through the ethical writings of Kant. The questions considered were virtually all shaped for us either by the utilitarianism of Bentham and Mill, or by G. E. Moore and his followers, who speculated endlessly and fruitlessly about the meaning of 'good', 'right' and 'ought', while confining their examples to such trivia of everyday life as would neutralise all desire for a moral solution. The manifest facts that modern man is living in a state of spiritual anxiety, that the world has become strange to us and frightening, that we lack and need a conception of our own existence – such facts went unnoticed in the prevailing moral philosophy. Ethics came to rest in the study of dilemmas, like that of the man who must visit his aunt in hospital on the very same day as his child is competing in the long-jump at school.

Continental philosophers have not neglected ethics. But from Hegel and Kierkegaard, through Schopenhauer and Nietzsche, to Sartre and Heidegger, they have shown a striking indifference to such everyday trivia, and concentrated instead on the position of the philosopher himself, in a world that is godless and unguided, and where we wander as strangers. The *real* problem, for such thinkers, is seldom encountered by the man in the street, even when both his aunt and his child are clamouring for his attention. The real problem comes into being only with the consciousness that discerns it, and this is a philosophical consciousness. Sartre and Heidegger offer a morality for the intellectual, in a world that denies him the possibility of religious faith. This explains the appeal of so much continental philosophy, and the disappointment of students with British philosophers, who seem to ignore entirely the thoughts and emotions that cause us to philosophize in the first place.

But here we encounter another peculiarly British trait. The concept of the intellectual, as a distinct human type, is absent from the mainstream of our philosophical culture. The British philosopher poses as a man of the people, motivated by ordinary concerns, whose scepticism is reserved for the metaphysicians, the mystics and the system-builders. Even when he is engaged, like Berkeley, in destroying the belief in a material reality, the British philosopher protests that he does so in the name of common sense, and in opposition to the outrageous paradoxism of his colleagues. Throughout the nineteenth century, when people of supreme intellectual accomplishment held the highest offices in Britain, it was never assumed that their education might in any way disqualify them from government, or induce the peculiar anti-bourgeois posture which was the perpetual theme of continental literature. Disraeli and Gladstone were regarded not as intellectuals, but as educated men, the more qualified for government on account of their literary achievements. Even those thinkers who felt some inkling of the spiritual vacancy of the modern world occupied

[handwritten: Thinkers used to persuade the common men to rise up to their level. Not no...]

their time, like Ruskin, in trying to persuade the man in the street to share their vision, or, like Morris, in dreaming of an idyllic union between the artist and the handyman.

The nearest our national culture has come to the concept of the intellectual is through Coleridge's theory of the clerisy – the class of thinking people who would perpetuate the spiritual and literary inheritance of the nation, and exert a permanent influence on government. Interestingly enough, it was Coleridge who led the reaction against British philosophy, repudiating, in the name of Kantian metaphysics, both the empiricist theory of knowledge, and the utilitarian theory of morality. Coleridge's complaints against Bentham were echoed in Matthew Arnold's defence of culture against the philistines, and in our own century by T. S. Eliot and F. R. Leavis, in their attempts to re-write the literary canon, and displace philosophy with poetry as the key to the modern condition.

If you are seeking for words to express and soothe the modern consciousness, you would certainly be disappointed by the works of British philosophers writing now, whose intellectual concerns are entirely remote from any recognisable human predicament. Their isolation from the surrounding culture is the price that British philosophers have paid for their obsession with valid argument – for validity is most easily achieved by saying nothing. Its greatest virtue – that it tries to say what it means and to mean what it says – is precisely what has unfitted British philosophy for survival in the modern world. The rival tradition, more literary than logical, which has its roots in nineteenth-century German romanticism, will always be more popular with the reading public. For it promises a philosophy of the modern condition itself.

[handwritten: Yes, that's the point of philosophy!]

Those words struck a chord with me, when I read them at the end of our supper. We had talked around the subject of philosophy throughout the meal, and Scruton had emphasized many times that he saw his own work as lying half in the British and half in the continental tradition. Like Sartre, he tells me, he believes that philosophy must make sense of the modern

[handwritten margin note: My preference]

condition, by engaging directly with *how it is for me*; in other words, with
the way things seem to someone who lives in a state of existential doubt. But
like Wiggins, Nagel, Kripke and others, he wishes to explore philosophical
ideas in the context of the scientific worldview. He refers at one point to the
famous article by Wilfrid Sellars on 'Philosophy and the Scientific Image
of Man', which he regards as a seminal attempt to put science in its proper
context, and also to rescue for philosophy a role in human understanding
that no other discipline might have. 'That work of rescue,' he tells me, 'is
what has motivated my writing in recent years, and especially the kind of
cognitive dualism that I develop in *The Soul of the World*. In the end, for all
my complaints, I remain in the tradition of British philosophy – or rather,
Anglophone philosophy, since the Americans have been very important to
me too – and can never really abandon the art of lucid thinking for the kind
of gobbledegook that creates such an impression when you stumble on it in
the works of Heidegger. I respect Heidegger's way of arguing. But it is a way
that shows no respect at all for the rest of us.'

I could do my
PhD with
- Newcastle
- Lancaster
Durham
- Lampeter

A continental focus,
and its 'use' in applying
to the human condition,
is important to me.

5

Eastern Europe

'I really enjoyed making life difficult for communists'

Roger Scruton gives concrete substance to his convictions and has often suffered as a result. This was most apparent in his work on behalf of the dissidents of Eastern Europe during their communist enslavement – work acknowledged by Václav Havel when in 1998, as president of the Czech Republic, he awarded Scruton the Medal for Merit (First Class) for his services to the Czech people, and also by the jury of the Lech Kaczyński Award, when they honoured Scruton in 2015 for his intellectual courage and friendship to Poland during the 1980s. In 2014, Scruton published a novel, *Notes from Underground*, in which he sought to evoke the strange, threatening and often surreal atmosphere of life under communist rule.[1] And his experience of those times has clearly shaped his consciousness in an unusual way.

Scruton has written about his experiences in Eastern Europe, but the essence of his opposition to communism is, in my view, best summed up in the closing paragraph of a lengthy essay he published on the French Revolution in 1989, the year that the communist order in Europe collapsed. 'Man's Second Disobedience' is Scruton at his Burkean best, a rebel against rebellion demonstrating that the 'first effect of the revolutionary mentality is to undo the experience of the sacred'. Whether that of France in 1789 or of Russia in 1917, revolution 'leads to murder, for the simple reason that it rids the world of the experience upon which the refusal to murder depends'. That is the experience of the incarnate person: the animal in whom the light of reason shines, and who looks at us with eyes which tell of freedom. Only now and then – in love, hatred and desire – does the reality of this incarnation overwhelm and trouble us. But the underlying sense of it is there in all respect, and all affection. It is this which forbids us to treat another's life and freedom as expendable, or to weigh his survival in the balance of our own individual profit. Our calculations stop short at the threshold of the other, precisely because his flesh is sanctified. The first effect of the revolutionary mentality is to undo this experience of the sacred. Once the idols have been brought to earth, individual freedom, and the flesh which harbours it, become *property*. They can be placed in the balance of calculation, and discarded 'for the public good'.[2]

In these lines, we see themes that would eventually form the basis of so much of Scruton's later thought – those of the *person*, freedom and the *sacred*. Indeed, his principal criticisms of pseudo-science and scientism – founded as they are on these three *transcendental* features of human experience – have also direct application to the 'politics' of revolution, as the final paragraph of 'Man's Second Disobedience' clearly illustrates:

In judging the revolutions of Europe, it is to the religion of Europe that we should turn. The Revolution is, I believe, a supreme act of Christian disobedience. Rather than worship a transcendental God, the revolutionary brings him down to earth, and reshapes him in the form of an ideal community. At once … God's face in the world is overcast and imperceivable. The worship of the idol becomes a worship of nothing – but it is a potent nothingness, which threatens everything real. It is the very same nothingness which, captured in a handkerchief, caused Othello to destroy the sacred thing which God had given him – and all for Nothing. As to what, or who, this nothing consists in, the question answers itself.[3]

This potent nothingness was something Scruton knew at first hand, and which planted a chill in his soul. But how did this transforming experience come his way? As we sit in his study, a world away from that of the communist dystopia, he explains: 'My friend Kathy Wilkes, who was an eminent philosopher and daughter of the Vicar of Marlow, who had prepared me for my Anglican confirmation, invited me to visit Julius Tomin's seminar in Prague in 1979. I had already agreed to address an aesthetics conference in Kraków, so I said that I would proceed from there to Prague. That was a big adventure for me. The Kraków conference was an international affair and I was excited because I had never been behind the Iron Curtain. Barry Smith, a dissident philosopher, who deserves far more recognition than he gets, and who is now editor of *The Monist* journal, had kept contact with people in Poland and Hungary because he shared their interest in Polish logic and phenomenology, and also in the aesthetician Roman Ingarden. So they invited Smith to come and I think he put my name forward as a possible speaker. It was an unforgettable experience.

'I was travelling with a German girl who had been brought up in East Germany and who wanted to revisit the communist devastation, so as "to know the place for the first time". We got off the plane in Warsaw in what looked and felt like a military airport, dimly lit and patrolled in every place by armed militia. We went through many customs barriers and passport controls only to discover that it was not possible to book a hotel, and that we had nowhere to go. Then someone buttonholed us, saying: "Come and stay in my place. I'll charge you five dollars each." We paid our five dollars and ended up in his apartment, which was totally bare except for beds. He lived with his wife and a small child in one corner of the place, keeping the rest of it unoccupied in the hope of bringing home some needy visitor from his regular visits to the airport. The flat was in a tall concrete block on the outskirts of Warsaw. There was an air of total destitution and poverty. The lights were burning low and there was very little heating. The following morning we were given breakfast, which consisted of ersatz coffee tasting of sawdust, and a raw onion. That was all he had. I wanted to see Warsaw, but to find a restaurant where there was anything to eat was all but impossible. And I think it was then that I first experienced the chill that haunted me henceforth until 1989, as though all that I encountered was a kind of mirage on the surface of a place composed of dark matter – a place totally unknowable to my previously trusted ways of finding my way about.

'At the conference they did have provisions of a rough-and-ready kind. It was a two-day conference and visitors were put up in the university, which was perfectly respectable. However, there was also an unofficial police force at the conference, mostly Bulgarians who were very obviously Party members. They would disrupt the discussion whenever it veered too far from Historical Materialism. One particular lady, dressed all in black, with huge broad shoulders and a beetle brow from which she looked downwards on us all, was vigilant throughout. She took issue with every ideological discrepancy. In the middle of a paper, she would suddenly throw up her head and shout: "Now this is not true! *Niejest prawda!*" And there would follow a strange demonization of the person who was speaking, and the ways in which he had deviated from the path of proletarian righteousness. If he was himself from a communist country he would pale and stammer to a halt, sometimes apologizing before returning to the thread of his argument.

'At that time, the Poles lived a double life. In the evenings, beautiful young people would walk arm in arm around the walls of Kraków, as though there were no trouble at all. They walked in a defiant way, with a sort of serenity of presence. It was just after Pope John Paul II had made his pilgrimage to Poland, so they were all buoyed up, and that was very moving to witness.

'After the conference, obedient to Kathy Wilkes's instructions, I set off to Prague on the train. It was a fascinating journey, ending in a private flat in Prague and a rather brusque encounter with the policemen who were guarding it. When I finally got through the door it was to confront a room full of people of all ages and of no profession, a gathering of prisoners who addressed me from silent suffering faces. That really did affect me, I have to say. It was like King Lear coming across Poor Tom! I was due to give a talk on Wittgenstein's 'Private Language' argument. Kathy told me to speak about that because she thought they would be fascinated by it, and they were. But I was more fascinated by the audience.

'My own involvement quickly became complicated. Two of the young people asked me if I would speak to them the next day about what really worried them, and what they were really interested in. They came to the assigned bench on Shooters Island in the Vltava – a boy and a girl – and explained the full extent of their problems since being thrown out of university for their anti-communist crimes. The girl, Lenka, made a plea to me to give thought to their situation and I said that I would. The spark that was lit between us then started something that burned low and constant over the next three years.'

It was from this experience that Scruton derived many of the details and some of the drama of his novel *Notes from Underground*, the genesis of which he explained in an article that appeared recently in the *Central and Eastern European London Review*:

As Spenser famously said in *The Faerie Queene*, the 'brave exploits which great Heroes won / In love were either ended or begun', and this is as true of the exploits achieved against nature by the timid as it is of those clocked up serenely by the brave. In my very first seminar in Prague I met a quiet, beautiful and poetic girl who, to my surprise, made it clear to me, through letters, that she would welcome another visit. I was still young, Lenka younger. And through her I got to know many of her contemporaries who had lost out on educational opportunities, careers, travel, and every kind of privilege because of the wrong thing said or done.

In Lenka's case the wrong thing was to have organized a reading group among students in her university dorm, in order to study the works of Kafka and Dostoyevsky. Others had been deprived of an education because their parents had signed Charter 77, or committed some other offence indicative of moral virtue in a world where nothing was a greater sign of unreliability than the disinterested desire to do good.

The thing that most vividly struck me about the young people I got to know was that they were not part of the 'dissident' world. You had to graduate to the status of dissident, and that involved being taken up by the Western media, being jailed from time to time, having the kind of signature that would create a stir when it appeared on an incriminating document. Dissidence was a social status like any other, and even if the price was one that most people were not prepared to pay, it brought order where there might have been chaos. Dissidence had a career structure, and your place in that structure gave meaning to your life and a reason for carrying on. It also brought fatigue and privations, and never has its atmosphere been so effectively caught as by Havel, in his play *Largo Desolato*, written in 1984, and first appearing in samizdat after my visits came to an end.[4]

So what happened to this relationship, and why did it lead to such a long-standing connection with the communist countries? Scruton explains: 'I went back to England quite shattered by the atmosphere. Kathy and I started talking about the whole thing. She had sent some other people over there, including the philosopher Anthony Kenny, who was arrested and then sent to the border. We all thought this was outrageous and that we should do something about it. Because I was interested in charity law, I drafted a document and proposed that we raise money to form a trust. In those days, you could do that without asking permission from the Charity Commissioners, who are a body of politically correct apparatchiks anyway. We got the trust established and raised money, not very much but enough to be able to buy books, plan some courses and begin recruiting visitors. Then Lenka came to England. She was travelling with a man who had permission to travel, and that marked him out as suspicious. But her intention was to visit me.

'We developed a correspondence and I still have her letters – very beautiful letters. I visited her and there was even a thought that we should get married. But it didn't work out because another young person in her circle intervened, saying that if she went to the West, and married me, that would be cowardice. It would be abandoning her country in its hour of need. That was the kind of consideration that weighed with Lenka, for whom public spirit and civil obligation have been the most important motives in her life, motives which can even be weighed against love. And of course, the person who gave her this advice married her.

'Before I finished *Notes from Underground* in 2013, I thought I should talk to her just to ensure that I wasn't going to be stirring up any trouble. So we arranged to meet and we are back on good terms, she now the mother of four children. When we met we were totally at ease with each other, as we had always been. She read *Notes from Underground* and said that it was a wonderful experience because, for her, it was coming home to what she had known. It *was* her experience. That made me very proud. But this is a digression.'

In the opening chapters of *Notes from Underground*, Scruton summons up the ghost of an almost forgotten past. In one evocative scene, he describes the underground life on the Prague Metro, which 'was a symbol of progress in a city whose beauty and antiquity were a standing offense to the proletarian future'. The protagonist continues:

The silence of our world was more intense underground. Even at rush hour, when the cars were full and people stood holding the handrails and staring past each other's ears, there was no noise apart from the roar of the train and the automated voice that told us that the doors were closing. Nobody exchanged greetings or apologies; no face smiled or departed in the slightest particular from the mask that everyone adopted, as the instinctive sign of a blameless inner emptiness, from which no forbidden thought could ever emerge.[5]

But was it really like that – like stepping into another world? 'Oh yes! It was the very thing that you had denied. You denied that such silence, such fear, such hopeless waiting existed on the other side of the curtain. Here we were in our comfortable Western democracy with our unreal battles. Well, they weren't really unreal, but they were battles that had a kind of theatrical aspect, and which could be lost without much pain. But over there, you met imprisoned people. It was like descending into Nibelheim, finding yourself in a dark place where you are the *only* free person. You are the only person who has the right to walk out of the door. It was both oppressive and inspiring, because people turned towards you faces of a kind you never see in your life here: faces full of suffering, longing to trust but never sure that they can. It had an erotic side to it, because only something like erotic love – something both egoistic and violently other-directed – can break through the barrier with which everyone tried to shield himself. However, as I try to convey in *Notes from Underground*, even that had been poisoned.'

How did it make Scruton feel, therefore, when he encountered Western intellectuals who adopted a pro-communist posture from the comfort and safety of their universities? 'It did make one realize how naïve those people are. But it also made me think of them as dangerous too, because all that we saw in Eastern Europe began with people like them: self-indulgent intellectuals like Lenin, with crazy ideas that he never thought through, pretending that the question before him was *purely* intellectual, and that he, with the big brain, will solve it. And then, when things get out of hand, saying, "Let's get rid of those people who are obstructing us." I think there is a moral obligation to denounce that way of thought for what it is. To be quite honest, at age seventy-one, with all my writing done, there is no cost to me in taking them on. Do I worry, for example, if all the lefties give my new edition of *Thinkers of the New Left* the same vitriolic reviews as last time? Probably I will be a bit upset, but I know that the book contains things that need to be said. And I am glad to be saying it.'

I remind Scruton that one major leftist did not come down on the side of the communists, but actually went to the aid of the same underground dissidents that Scruton helped in Prague. Jacques Derrida, intellectual superstar and founder of what we have come to know as 'deconstruction', helped establish the Jan Hus Educational Foundation in 1981 – a group that provided help for persecuted Czech intellectuals and of which he eventually became vice-president. Derrida's biographer Geoffrey Bennington describes what happened when Derrida travelled to Prague to run a 'clandestine seminar' in the same year:

> [Derrida is] followed for several days, stopped at the end of the week, finally arrested at the airport, and, after a police operation on his suitcase in which they pretend to discover a brown powder, he is imprisoned on the charge of 'production and trafficking of drugs'. Signature campaign for his release. Released ('expelled') from Czechoslovakia after an energetic intervention of François Mitterrand and the French government.[6]

I inform Scruton that Derrida was in fact imprisoned for three days, during which he shared a cell with a drunken gypsy, to which he responds: 'Well, that's splendid!'

Scruton has been a consistent critic of Derrida's writing and influence. In a lecture delivered at the University College of Swansea in 1993, he wrote:

> What deconstruction sets before us is a profound mystery, which can be approached only through the incantation of invented words, through a Newspeak which deconstructs its own meaning in the act of utterance. When at last the veil is lifted, we perceive a wondrous landscape: a world of negations, a world in which, wherever we look for presence we find absence, a world not of people but of vacant idols, a world which offers, in the places where we seek for order, friendship and moral value, only the skeleton of power. There is no creation in this world, though it is full of cleverness – a cleverness actively deployed in the cause of Nothing.[7]

Now, however, he tells me of his admiration for what Derrida did for a cause which transcends any intellectual dispute. 'The philosopher Alan Montefiore, who was sympathetic to Derrida, was also part of our circle – his wife set up the French branch of the Jan Hus Educational Foundation so that we could cooperate. That was very useful to us because it meant that we weren't typecast as English imperialists. In my opinion, the best thing that Derrida ever did was to get arrested in Prague. It was great that *he* in particular got detained because it was his reality moment, and also the Czech security service's reality moment. They had not done their homework. They knew they were going to arrest our next visitor, and it turned out to be Derrida. If they had arrested me on that occasion, I would probably have languished in some prison and not been regretted! But arresting a leftist celebrity, personal friend of the French president, was just the biggest mistake they could have made! It was wonderful because after that they hesitated to touch us.'

I interject to remind Scruton that Derrida described his experience in a Czech jail as 'Kafkaesque', an irony considering he went to Prague to research and lecture on Kafka. Following his release, Derrida also declared that 'until one is touched by something like this one cannot imagine what a paradise of liberty we live in', to which Scruton responds: 'Yes, he was mugged by reality, and I only wish it had happened to more of his colleagues. That was my experience through Lenka: through her, I knew the inside of the planned Utopia and I felt exactly as Derrida did. I was probably as much improved by Lenka and the trauma she caused as Derrida was improved by that drunken gypsy.'

I ask Scruton if, having battled for so many years against an evil empire that showed no signs of crumbling, at any stage he foresaw the events of 1989 when the communist order collapsed. 'No, I didn't. I thought this was going to go on forever and that we would succumb too. And maybe we will succumb, though it will be to something rather different under Mr Putin. Nevertheless, at first I was overjoyed in 1989. After my arrest in 1985 I had not been able to go to the Czech lands. I could visit Poland and Hungary, but I was always followed in Poland. Then after 1989 everything was free again. I actually went to Moscow in 1989 when Mikhail Gorbachev was in office. There was certainly a sense that things were moving. However, I was *so* suspicious: after all, you don't become president of the Soviet Union just by being a decent guy or having an idea about how to liberate the country. You get there through the KGB network.

'And here is the funny thing. Communism is through and through dependent on paranoia – a kind of grand conspiracy theory designed to manufacture illusory enemies so as to maintain itself in being. And you respond in kind. You too become paranoid and see in everything a conspiracy instead of a cock-up. I came to think that the KGB had perceived that they could achieve what they really wanted without the tiresome business of oppression: first by stealing everything and putting it in Swiss bank accounts; second, by building up their networks abroad so as to continue enjoying the good life and forgetting about Russia. They're all in London now, having moved their assets and become legitimate global oligarchs who are only occasionally obliged to put poison in each other's drinks. It may not be necessary after all to pickle the entire Russian population in gulags. You can get enormous IMF funds by pretending to free the Russian people, even if you are only freeing yourself. Remember, the IMF poured masses of money into the Soviet Union after 1990, and this money subsequently ended up in Swiss bank accounts controlled by Putin and his people.'

I ask if he believes that this realization by the KGB would have happened without Gorbachev. 'I don't know, but I enjoy my little paranoid fantasy. You know, I ponder these things often and never come up with a clear answer. What I do believe, however, is that, as Nietzsche said, resentment is the default position of a social animal. It was resentment that produced the communist movement and the revolution to which it led, and you see this, for example, in the Czech lands today. Of course, my circle of Czech friends is now comparatively prosperous and middle-class. They are people who don't live by the rule of resentment. They are mostly religious and accepting of the new position of the Czech Republic, although not happy with the corrupting influence exerted by the EU, which offers real rewards for unreal attitudes, and relentlessly opposes the values for which they stood up under communism, which are the values of national independence and cultural integrity.

'Although I don't believe the story of original sin in its literal reading, I nevertheless recognize that it contains a profound truth about humanity, which is that all our efforts are, in the end, poisoned by our inheritance, because that inheritance is what we are. We compete for the basic things and for recognition, and in every new circumstance this means that the old relations of domination will be reproduced, but in different forms. I think one should stop hoping for anything else. That is the great message of Wagner's *Ring* cycle and it is why I am currently writing a book about it. The rescue doesn't come from the public sphere but from within, when you recognize that *you* must renounce your bids for power and domination, and that the moments of love are the only things that were really given to you. We don't find it easy to accept this, because it demands so much of us – that we cease resenting others, and cease laying claim to what we have done nothing to deserve.'

The dissidents emerged from their catacombs and many became leaders of their newly liberated countries. How did this make Scruton feel? 'It was lovely at first, but I knew they were incompetent! After the collapse, I spent a few months in Czechoslovakia trying to transfer the assets of our charity to Brno. We were the first registered charity in Moravia and I was trying to get our people there to set an example, by helping the universities and the schools to enter the new world of opportunity. However, everything was *totally* ruined. The universities were as my left-wing colleagues would like them to be here – uniformly dreary and governed by resentment, with second-rate people giving lectures to bewildered students about the need to impose a regime of equality on them all.

'I had worked for a while in the underground with Jiří Müller, who had been foreman in a fire extinguisher factory, before being arrested in 1968 and spending the next five years in prison. Afterwards, he had worked for the destruction of the communist system, totally secretly, and was very hard to know. But I managed to get through to him and became just about the only foreigner he trusted. In the early 1980s we had worked closely together on samizdat publication, on setting up a network to support schools which would teach Czech literature and history as they should be taught, on little community ventures involving both the Lutheran and Catholic churches, and on anything else that could contribute to keeping the Czech identity alive. A communism-free zone, in other words.

'He himself was a social democrat. Like so many Czechs, the political choice for him was what it had been in the aftermath of Nazism – totalitarian socialism on the one hand, or social democracy on the other. I was with him when I was arrested, and he was very clear about what his rights were. He said, "Look, my guest has to go back to my house to pick up his stuff." So we drove to his house in his chugging Tatra pursued by two vast Mercedes. They let us go in together, and surrounded the house outside. We stood in the bathroom, out of sight of all the windows, as he systematically ate the things I'd given him – messages, lists and a whole lot of other bits! In a way, it was quite amusing. I was taken away and interrogated, but allowed back to Jiří's house, from where he drove me to the border, still pursued by the spooks in their Mercedes. I couldn't return to the Czech lands for another five years, though it did not matter so much, since we had built a fairly impregnable network by then.

'The next time I saw Jiří was post-1989. He had been appointed head of the Secret Police for Moravia. He was the person responsible for seeing that this mess didn't occur again, that everything would be normalized and that the Secret Police would be permanently disbanded. He was in the office of the Secret Police in Prague seated at a big desk in his open-necked shirt and rolled-up sleeves with people in uniform standing, silent and stony-faced, behind him. I said, "Well, it's great to see you in this office!" to which he immediately replied, "Shush! If you have any particular messages write them here", pushing a little notepad across to me. So I wrote little messages to him and he put them into his shirt pocket ready to eat them again. He didn't keep that job for long.'

And what of Scruton's award from President Havel, the most famous of all former dissidents, for his services to the Czech people? Was it an endorsement of all he did during the dark years? 'I was very pleased, of course! One is always grateful for such things. Honours are controversial, especially in Britain where they are offered, as a rule, to other members of the clique in power, in order to reinforce its own social status, as Eric Hobsbawm was made Companion of Honour after all those years of work on behalf of the Soviet Union. But over there for a while the people able to confer the honours were those who themselves deserved them. So they knew the distinction between honour and dishonour – indeed, they had lived by it. I hadn't known President Havel and I had only an indirect relationship with the Charter 77 group, of which he was a leading member. Of course, the Charter was truly important, both as a symbol and as a cover. The attention and malice of the Secret Police were largely focused on the Charter signatories. In the shadows created by that illuminated battle other things could grow unobserved.'

I turn to the figure of Jan Patočka, Czech philosopher and first spokesman for Charter 77. On the night of 3 March 1977, he was arrested and interrogated for ten hours. Patočka became ill while in custody and was taken to hospital. He died on 13 March aged sixty-nine. I ask Scruton if Patočka was a martyr for the resistance. 'Yes. I think Havel had asked him to be the first spokesman of Charter 77, and he had accepted without wanting to make any fuss about it. He thought that it was his duty. The Helsinki Accords were, after all, legal, and their ratification meant that they were part of the law of Czechoslovakia too – in so far as a communist country could have a rule of law. He was a frail old man – although only my age, and I don't feel like a frail old man. In those countries at that time, people aged rather more rapidly. Anyway, they treated him very cruelly: interrogating and interrogating until eventually he died of a brain haemorrhage.

'I was actually very inspired by Patočka's underground lectures. We had a service run out of the Institut für die Wissenschaften vom Menschen (Institute for Human Sciences) in Vienna, where I had befriended a brave and good man called Klaus Nellen, who acted as a messenger. He made contact with the Patočka archive and made it his business to bring out the many typescripts one by one. We accumulated quite a lot of Patočka's writings, despite all the difficulties. I read the lectures on Plato and Europe.[8] They were beautiful in a way – both naïve, as though Plato's theory of the republic can really address the situation in Europe now, and also full of allusions to the trauma of Central Europe, which so few in the West have really appreciated. They were written in a lucid, fluent Czech, which I could read without too much difficulty. And that made me think that he had absolutely the right approach for the people, like Havel, who attended his seminars – namely, to present his wealth of philosophical knowledge in a simple way while addressing the issues that are ours now.

'Patočka was a pupil of Edmund Husserl, and he thought, with the later Husserl, that the modern world has witnessed a complete transformation of the subjectivity of human beings. We no longer experience our own being in the way of our ancestors. We don't experience our being as a religious believer in the eighteenth or nineteenth century would have experienced it, or even as a natural patriot of the old world would have experienced it. We experience it as something fragmented and threatened. But we have, nevertheless, the same need for community as people in other times. We confront the mass murders and mass destructions of the twentieth century, knowing that we are part of this and also entirely alienated by it. From this, a new kind of solidarity is born – a solidarity of people who are fragmented, shattered and who have to put themselves together anew.

'One reason for thinking Patočka is right, is that people now living in the West do not have the yearning for community which is the natural human condition. They need community, but cannot desire it, since it seems to take away so much from their individual comforts. Community means being uninsured against the future: it means giving, losing, pouring out, becoming undefended. How far this is from the comforts that we are promised by the all-powerful state! Thus the Labour Party fights the election saying that "we're going to offer you *more* of a National Health Service". That is what government is about: maintaining you in an amniotic bath from birth to grave. There is no need for you to have loving relations with anyone or to make a sacrifice for anyone but yourself. All that matters is to be maintained in your self-centred isolation in such a way that the body does not give out. Patočka would have seen in this another sign of the "solidarity of the shattered".

I interrupt to say that people in Patočka's world realized they were in a fragmented state, but that we don't seem to realize it in our world. Self-knowledge, Scruton responds, 'is such a rare achievement. But let me go back to what Derrida said regarding the paradise of liberty we live in. In the end, I suppose, the most important thing is that one has the freedom to live in another way. The people in Patočka's world were looking for that freedom and they didn't find it. But in the looking for it, they had a vision which perhaps we should envy: they imagined the elsewhere place that one day they would stumble across, where their eyes would be open to other eyes that looked on them with love and forgiveness. That was a real experience in those days, and especially in Poland, as I often observed. And it is a theme that I explore in *Notes from Underground*'.

I ask him if he is proud about his work in Eastern Europe. 'To be quite honest, there was nothing to be proud of. I really enjoyed making life difficult for communists! It was a great pleasure in itself. I worried about people and had lots of sleepless nights when my contacts were arrested. But I wouldn't say I was *proud* of it. It was just something I did and what I did was totally secret and private and nothing was ever said about it, at least not by me. My approach was that this is something we're doing and it would be great if it succeeded in any way, but it will probably fail. Either way, let's just keep on doing it and not talk about it. We were really strict about not giving any information.'

Scruton often drew attention to those he believed to be the true heroes in the struggle against the communists. In 1985, the same year he was arrested and banned from the Czech lands, Scruton used his column in *The Times* to write a tribute to the signatories of Charter 77, including Jan Patočka, whom he referred to as 'the greatest luminary of modern Czech culture'. In countering the 'benighted paranoia' of the Prague regime which wishes 'its citizens to live in a state of war', Scruton wrote that 'Charter 77 continues to make the only real contribution to peace that has originated in communist Czechoslovakia since 1968. By reminding us that a government can be at peace with its neighbours only if it is first at peace with its subjects, and by showing peace to be inseparable from the rule of law, it provides a lesson not only to the authorities in Prague but also to the world.'[9]

In fact Scruton was privately doing much more than making life difficult for communists. Later in the evening, over dinner, he tells me a remarkable story which he has never put on the record before now. 'When you get involved in difficult and precarious ventures like those that led me into Eastern Europe, your life is often changed in quite unforeseeable ways. I even managed to acquire a kind of family as a result. It happened this way. Around 1981 or 1982, Jessica Douglas-Home approached me because she was anxious about the power of the Communist Party, the support it received from Western intellectuals and the seeming permanence of its ambitions. It was the time of the Peace Movement, the Greenham Common Peace Camp and the Campaign for Nuclear Disarmament. So there was, in the air, a new sense of threat, not only that the Soviet machine was active and looking for opportunities, but also that the conflict was alive in the West. There was a conflict between the Peace Movement and the established principles of NATO and Western foreign policy. And this was particularly vivid in Britain, especially following the Soviet invasion of Afghanistan in 1979. Jessica's husband Charlie had been a reporter in Czechoslovakia at the time of the Soviet invasion in 1968, and he had a clear vision of what the post-war settlement was really about – a vision that influenced his work as editor of *The Times*, and which had profoundly influenced Jessica too. When she came to see me it was with the determination to do something by way of supporting movements of resistance in Eastern Europe. I said she should study the methods we had used in Czechoslovakia, but that it had to be done very carefully and slowly. She agreed and joined our trust. Then she and I and Caroline Cox decided to set up another trust for Poland and Hungary: The Jagiellonian Trust, which was founded on the model of the Jan Hus Educational Association, but in completely different circumstances. It was much easier to get in and out of those countries, and the universities had not suffered the purge that had been inflicted on the universities in Czechoslovakia. So to some extent, at least, one could operate through dissident sections within the universities. We got things going, recruiting Marek Matraszek, Dennis O'Keeffe and Tim Garton Ash as trustees, and Caroline simultaneously set up a medical relief operation. She used to drive lorries there with all the medicines that were needed. So our network in Poland was quite extensive, though without the concentrated intellectual core of the Czech operation.

'At a certain stage, Jessica, who is a singularly intrepid person, decided that it was all pointless if we couldn't include Romania. I said you can do that if you like, but I have enough on my plate. And to my astonishment she did! She set up a little trust for Romania, started working with Romanian exiles in London and meeting the dissidents in Romania, which was a very hard and dangerous thing. You had to work very carefully through people you could trust in the West, who would give you addresses to which you had to go at a certain hour and with certain expectations and explanations. Messages had to be in code, you had to carry nothing suspicious, never leave anything in your hotel room and not do anything foolish like take off your jacket in a restaurant where the pockets might be emptied as you ate your food.

'Anyway, she got it going and I was full of admiration. The boys whom I used as messengers to Poland and Hungary became keen and took messages to Romania as well. At one stage Jessica put together an event in London, involving exiles from Poland, Hungary and Romania, and designed to draw attention to the situation in those countries and the need to offer help. In relation to this event I was deputed to discuss publicity with Iolanda Stranescu, who was a leading member of the Romanian resistance in London. She had already heard from Jessica that I had horses, and had talked to her children about it. As we were conducting our business, Christina, her eight-year-old and eldest daughter, came in and, without saying anything, stood silently in the doorway dressed for horse riding in boots and cap. I asked if she'd like to come and ride a horse. Her response was '*Quand? Après l'école ce vendredi?*' I took her down that weekend and within a few weeks she had adopted me, and included her sisters too in the deal.

'Their father had left and there was a real question about what was going to happen to these three little girls. Now they had hit on the perfect solution, which was to find a middle-aged bachelor who didn't have any dependants and to install themselves in his country cottage at weekends! I saw them through their education, and Sophie and the children now regard them as part of our family. Christina is married, with a child, and teaching science in a Leeds comprehensive. I have to say that this second-hand family has been a great joy to me, and not the least of the unexpected benefits that have flowed from my interest in Eastern Europe.'

In his quiet yet determined way, Roger Scruton had rescued a family from what was, perhaps, the most benighted country in Eastern Europe and changed the course of their lives forever, offering them the opportunities that so many were denied in their homeland. I recall reading his tribute to the 'Pony Club' in *News from Somewhere*, which, as he wrote, opens a door 'into the mysterious forms of membership that characterise rural life'. But the particular passage that I recall is this:

> Every Summer, during the last week of July, we share in the excitement of the 'Camp', as one or other of our protégées goes through her paces, earning badges, rosettes and status, and returning each day with new friends, new skills and new knowledge. Our protégées are the children of Romanian refugees: but the Pony Club has fully acclimatised them to England; they understand the reticence, the formality, the uncompromising tolerance and the need to be tough; most of all they understand and identify with the resolute independence of spirit that has been destroyed in their homeland but which still lives around here.[10]

I now realize that those children were Christina and her sisters, Scruton's 'adopted family' as it were. When I remind him of that poignant passage, he remarks that 'the correct attitude to immigrants and refugees is not to crowd them into ghettos, but to integrate them into your way of life, since it is the most precious thing you have and the thing that they must adopt if they are not be a threat to the civil order. So Christina and her sisters received the full immersion treatment from me.'

Scruton's attitude to communism and its victims contrasts rather vividly with the many who, from the comfort of Western universities, took the side of the Soviet Union. Indeed, Scruton proceeds to tell me that, in response to the activities on behalf of the Soviets by 'fellow travellers' within the universities, 'I started a little institution called "Dons for Defence". It was an attempt to get as many academics as possible to speak out against the so-called Peace Movement, to sign letters in response to the fellow travellers' abundant letters to the press and to issue declarations and information when called upon. We smuggled articles from Eastern Europe berating the Peace Movement for its naivety, and these articles, although necessarily anonymous, had a great effect when published in *The Times*. When people understood that you can demonstrate against nuclear weapons in the West, but end up in the gulag if you do so in the East, they began to understand the difference between the two regimes, and the true source of the belligerence. Through this network I worked with some truly excellent people – sociologists like Christie Davies and the late David Levy, as well as the sprinkling of colleagues who had not joined the other side. We even set out to undo some of the work of the "peace studies" movement, that had its own university department in Bradford, and that too led me into deep waters. So yes, those were interesting times.'

6

Why Architecture?

'Real architecture is getting beyond the shed'

It is Palm Sunday and British Summer Time has just begun. Before we head to church, I ask Scruton about one of his central and abiding concerns: architecture. He has published two books on the subject: *The Aesthetics of Architecture* in 1979 and *The Classical Vernacular*[1] in 1994. Throughout his career, he has also published countless articles and papers on architectural principles, one of which was his second column written for *The Times* on 18 January 1983. Entitled 'Against Architecture' – although it would have been better named 'Against Architects' – it captures the essence of Scruton's understanding of building and why he believes it should be a pivotal philosophical preoccupation:

We must begin by destroying the illusion that architects are necessary. Architecture, like clothing, is a vernacular art. It provides predictable answers to predictable problems. Architects have conned us into an exaggerated view of their significance. Sometimes they produce wonderful things. But for the most part they are as dispensable as dress designers, and far more dangerous... Buildings no more have specific functions than do clothes. All successful buildings are, like Covent Garden or the lofts of Lower Manhattan, infinitely adaptable, precisely because they address themselves not to specific functions but to the general and vacillating requirements of human existence. First among these requirements – as the example of clothing displays – is an appearance of order, agreeableness and normality. Architects must understand appearances, not functions. Until they do so they are no better qualified than anyone else.[2]

When, however, did Scruton first become interested in this subject? 'I suppose it was when we had moved to Marlow when I was sixteen, and I had got to know Bob, Isabel, Bron and Francesca – the bohemian family about whom I spoke earlier. Marlow was then a really pretty little town on the banks of the River Thames, with a lovely high street of seventeenth- and eighteenth-century houses built around an old brewery and leading to a gothic revival church beside the river. The developers were moving in, pulling these things down and replacing them with faceless structures of concrete and glass. I suffered this as a personal pain – I think we all did.

'At the time, all sensitive English people felt that something dreadful was happening to their country. Later generations have become slightly inured to it, since they don't know what had disappeared before their time, and don't feel quite so bereft. For me, it wasn't just that something valuable was being swept away, but more importantly that those responsible had no idea what to put in its place. I had a sense that the cause of the destruction was not economic necessity, but ignorance. There was something to be known about how things fit together, how a street must look and how one creates a shared settlement. And that knowledge had gone.

'That thought was in my mind as a teenager and I started meditating about it later when I had studied aesthetics. After I published *Art and Imagination* in 1974, I was considering what should be my next task. It seemed a good idea to apply the kind of aesthetic thinking that I had been defending to the knowledge that was being so palpably lost from architectural practice. So I wrote *The Aesthetics of Architecture*, trying to start from first principles. I pointed out that judgement in architecture is not just a matter of taste like a taste in food. Judgement has to do with our understanding of human communities and of human freedom. It has to do with what we create in creating a shared environment. Essentially we create ourselves – we realize ourselves as rational, social beings. That

was when I became interested in the Hegelian idea of the *Entäusserung* –
the outward realization of the inner life. The most important aspect of
Entäusserung is our attempt to confer permanence on our condition as
free beings – to set free choice in stone. That is what architecture is, or
ought to be.'

I ask Scruton if it was ideology or ignorance that led British planners to
vandalize places like Marlow. 'It was both. Ideology drives out knowledge.
It creates a sense of urgency and self-appointed virtue, which forbids the
ideologue from consulting those who know. I was only a child, but post-war
Europe – as I saw it then – was not just a devastated continent with huge
problems of housing. It was also a guilt-ridden civilization in a posture of
repudiation towards its own past. After two wars, people had lost confidence
in their values, and buildings were the most important and unavoidable
symbol of those values, which had been bequeathed by the past. Our old
buildings were witnesses to damaged ideals and it was necessary to obliterate
their message.

'If you combine those two things – the political need for massive
redevelopment and the posture of repudiation towards the past – you open
the way to the socialist approach to planning. You wish then to sweep away
the clutter and create new settlements, in which the old hierarchies cannot
grow, and where all the residents will be treated equally. That is a respectable
frame of mind, but it is based on ignorance – ignorance of human
nature, and of what can be achieved by planning. The planners had been
encouraged by architectural modernism, by the founder of the Bauhaus
school Walter Gropius and the Swiss-French architect Le Corbusier, for
whom the architect is not just a craftsman but a social engineer, someone
who is reorganizing society from above. They believed that they had all the
answers and that people were wrong in wanting what *they* wanted. People
had to be gathered up and organized in a way that only Gropius and Le
Corbusier understood.'

The Aesthetics of Architecture was written very differently from *Art and
Imagination*. It was, for a start, more Hegelian and less analytical in tone
and content. It also anticipated the approach and style that would become
commonplace in Scruton's writings down the decades. Consider, for

example, this paragraph in the concluding chapter to that book, entitled 'Architecture and Morality':

> Self-realisation requires then that the agent have some real sense, in the present, of his continuity into the future. His future satisfactions must in some way enter into his present calculations, even though they are not the objects of present desire. Until he has achieved that rational balance between himself at one time and himself at another, he lives as it were expended in the present moment. But what makes this achievement possible? On the idealist view art, and the aesthetic impulse, play an important part in the process of 'spreading oneself' on the objective world. The view gains support from our reflections on the art of building. The process of 'self-realisation', of breaking from the prison of immediate desire, is a kind of passage from subject to object, a making public and objective of what is otherwise private and confused. But someone can set foot on the ladder of self-realisation only when he has some perception of its reliability, and this cannot be achieved by subjective fiat. He must first find himself at home in the world, with values and ambitions that are shared. He must be able to perceive the ends of his activity not in himself but outside himself, as proper aims in a public world, endowed with a validity greater than the validity of mere 'authentic' choice.[3]

I ask Scruton to explain how he approached this book, one which was so clearly different from anything that came before. 'I had read the works of architectural theory used by Sir Nikolaus Pevsner and others, who had set out to ideologize the post-war rebuilding of Britain. Almost everything I read seemed like a self-serving apology for the worst forms of vandalism, with no understanding of what is at stake when we build a shared public space. So I set out to refute the old theories about space and function, and to begin, philosophically, from first principles, showing the role of the imagination in our understanding of architectural detail. I argued that our perception of architecture is not a perception of its utility, that form does not follow function, that we relate to the built environment in something like the way we relate to each other and that successful architecture will always bear the marks of a community, conceived as an end in itself.

'People didn't understand *Art and Imagination* because it was written analytically and therefore in another language from that used by the art critics. However, *The Aesthetics of Architecture*, which was published by Princeton University Press, has been a continuous seller, recently reissued but never out of print. It was greeted with a barrage of hostility from the architects, but taken to their hearts by people in obscure places who had been battling for years against the nonsense. It addressed, for them, the most important issue, which is why does architecture matter so much, and why are we suffering from the uglification of our world? I have recently been in lengthy correspondence with an architect in Syria, Marwa al-Sabouni, who has been inspired by the book to develop her own train of argument, detailing the contribution of architectural vandalism to the destruction of her country. Her very moving book about this will be published next year by Thames & Hudson.'

And what of his second book on architecture, *The Classical Vernacular*: how does Scruton assess that work now? 'It is not really a book of philosophical aesthetics. It is much more a work of criticism, taking individual issues and producing a response to them. It is rather more poetic than *The Aesthetics of Architecture*, and attempts to place architecture in the context of the city, as the greatest human enterprise after farming – the second step that we took from the world of the hunter-gatherer, and which we took in trepidation and relying always on the help of our gods.'

In a chapter of *The Classical Vernacular* entitled 'Architecture and the *Polis*', Scruton speaks of 'sacred architecture', writing that:

Settlement is a communal act. Only where people can associate and reproduce, will a settlement be more than a camp. And the idea of community will be in the minds of those who build: their activity will be a communal enterprise. For they are laying claim to the land and protecting what they see as *ours*. The place chosen will be a sacred place. Even if it has not yet been favoured by the gods, it will become so through the very fact that *we* have chosen it. In the natural conditions of hardship the gods travel with us as our protectors, and endorse those ties of membership that enable us to survive amid our foes. The primary forms of architecture will therefore be sacred: the forms of the temples where the gods reside.[4]

He expands on these ideas in a new introduction to *The Aesthetics of Architecture*, which was reissued by Princeton University Press in 2013:

The classical Orders are extrapolated from the sacred architecture of the ancient world. Their peculiar authority comes not from subsequent history only, but from their original use. From the concept of the temple, permeable to the city, yet sacred and removed from it, came that of the colonnade, and thence of the single column as the unit of meaning. The Roman building types – arch, aedicule, engaged column, pilaster, vault and dome – can all be seen as attempts to retain the sacred presence of the column, in the full context of civic life. In them we see the interpenetration of the sacred and the secular, and thus the sanctifying of ordinary humanity, and the humanising of the divine. That is the source of their appeal, and the reason for their durability. With the Roman building types began the true history of European architecture, which is the history of the *implied Order*. We see this Order preserved in doors and windows, in mouldings and cornices all across the Western world, and in the old forms of Islamic architecture too ... Hence, prior to the modernist revolution, architects and builders have always used sacred shapes and details, in order to accommodate facade to facade, window to window and doorway to doorway along a street, and thereby to make that street into a public space.

I think it is important to remember this when we address the question of how to build today. The modern city street is composed from forms that have never had a sacred use or played a role in consecrating the land. They do not bear the imprint of those primal fears and needs from which gods are born. The new city is a city in which glazed facades mirror each other's emptiness across streets that die in their shadow. The facelessness of such a city is also a kind of godlessness.

Those ideas form the basis of Scruton's conservative and religious outlook as discussed in many subsequent works. I ask when the idea of the sacred origins of architecture first struck him. 'I was quite influenced at a certain stage by the British architect Quinlan Terry, with whom I used to discuss these matters. He is a passionate, evangelical Christian, who takes very seriously the story that, on Mount Sinai, God gave to Moses not just the Ten Commandments and the law, but also the design for a temple – a temple built with columns and architraves. He has the eccentric but interesting view that the classical idiom is of divine inspiration. Whatever you think of that, Quinlan is surely right that the building of a temple is the first step towards undertaking the communal task of settling. It is a consecration of the land, and a bid for a home.

'Different peoples have different gods and rituals, but the first step towards settling is to make a home for the god. That is because the god *is* the spirit of your community and the thing that protects you, the thing that reminds you that you are together and under a shared obedience. All those are matters that are wound into our social nature. So, if you can't build a temple and get it right, all other building is merely provisional and utilitarian. It becomes a matter of putting up sheds. Real architecture is precisely getting beyond the shed to the settlement, in which the earth is transformed from a mere habitat to a lasting habitation. This we see wonderfully accomplished in Venice, which is a lasting work of the religious imagination, a vision of eternity rising like Venus from the sea.

'Now, it is also true that buildings can perpetuate the idea of the temple without there being one, which is essentially what the classical idiom did. If you look at a place like Bath, it radiates in every way the idea of a legitimate settlement, showing people living side by side and protected. That is partly because it is built in stone, but more importantly because it is built to stand in just the way that temples stand. And that's the gift of the classical orders. Marwa beautifully illustrates in her book what has happened to the urban fabric of Syria, where the shared vocabulary of the old Islamic architecture, taken from church and mosque and developed as a street-by-street blessing of the land, has been replaced by a routine and caricature version, stuck like a label onto concrete structures that bear no relation to the land and its past. From the materialist Babylon of Dubai to the concrete rubble of the destroyed Syrian cities we see what architectural modernism has meant for the Middle East, and if you study Le Corbusier's plan for Algiers (or rather, for the destruction of Algiers) you will understand the contempt for man and God that lies at the heart of the modernist vision.'

Before moving to the country, Scruton lived in London. I enquire if he noticed the slow desecration of that city which was once a model of classical order and of the kind of consecration of the land that he advocates. 'The Ryans – the family that I met in Marlow – were connected to a bohemian circle of the previous generation from mine. They were the sort of people who were described by Evelyn Waugh: naughty, witty and frightfully well connected. As I said earlier, they were the kind of people who would inherit fortunes, spend them in a week and end up on the bottom until the next fortune came along. But one of these people, Madge Roeber, took me in when I began my wanderings. Her daughter Johanna, who is still a friend and was also a friend of Bron, had been brought up on the farm that Madge had run in the war as part of the war effort. Madge had an apartment in a big house in Hamilton Terrace; arriving from High Wycombe I was struck by the extraordinary peace of St John's Wood. It was like visiting the countryside after life in a Manchester slum – the very experience that my father once had, and which turned him towards marriage and settling down. There were wide streets along which a car would occasionally purr, views of gardens and trees, the sound of birdsong, and, lining the streets, houses with beautiful porches and elegant sash windows, turning their smiling faces to the day. People would walk in a dignified way and they dressed so well! They seemed to put a great effort into looking right before they went outside their houses. Madge's apartment was a haven for me. I had never been to a place like that – a place of peace and quiet and comfort – and her protective attitude to me was a great moral resource in my early troubles.

'I suppose I owe to Madge the sense that there is another kind of idyll than the one that had enchanted my father. The countryside never lost its appeal for me. Nevertheless, after I had discovered London I felt that real peace, real order and real protection are gifts of the city. That is where civilization begins and ends. Such was London in those days, before the hideous destruction of its skyline by childish skyscrapers and before its social transformation into a hectic airport terminal. The only job I could get, aged seventeen, and the only place I could live in, were in the East End, which was different from Madge's street but not *so* different. Mile End Road, Bethnal Green and Stepney Green had been very heavily bombed, but not so heavily that there weren't fine Georgian streets remaining – such as the one in which I was staying in a house full of dropouts and weirdos.

'In those days the East End was the heart of a working-class community. People would gather in the pubs on a Friday and Saturday, the men bringing their wives for a night out. They would all look smart: the men would wear suits and ties and their wives would doll themselves up. And they would sing. Sometimes they would have a "knees up" or one of the men would dress in drag and croon out war-time songs, full of a plaintive nostalgia for the time when they stood together against the common enemy. It was an old working-class celebration, much as George Orwell would have described it. At the Three Crowns in Stepney (which closed in 2010) there was a piano and sometimes I played it because there was no one else to do so – though I have always been hopeless without sheet music.

'Eventually, that all faded away but it was not German bombardment that destroyed the East End. It was, first of all, the mania for slum clearance, which meant sweeping away beautiful streets and replacing them with towers of concrete. Slum clearance was a conspiracy between planners schooled in the mad theories of Gropius, architects who were making a fortune and socialists who saw an unrivalled way to create obedient and equal citizens out of the unruly raw material of old England. The English working class fled because they couldn't live in the environment that their enlightened betters provided for them. Indigenous industries fled too, and in came the immigrants, who wander in the ruined wastes of Tower Hamlets nursing in their hearts the image of the other, better and more godly place to which they really belong, but whose non-existence has yet to be explained to them.'

Given all that Britain has gone through, and given how much it has changed demographically and architecturally, have Scruton's views on building changed since the publication of *The Aesthetics of Architecture* in 1979? 'Not my views on architecture. Unlike Quinlan Terry, I don't believe that the classical style is the only possible style. But I do think that there are universal principles which, though not *a priori* valid, express the ongoing consensus of mankind. Buildings should stand up. They should have a vertical emphasis and not be built out of horizontal planes. To recognize this is a huge step already, because it condemns the axonometric way of designing buildings that has been the norm – though a norm that is giving way to the even more appalling computer-designed gadgets of Rem Koolhaas and Zaha Hadid. I think buildings should have significant details, derived from a proper syntax and vocabulary, and that lines – especially lines which are borders or edges – should have mouldings so as to collect shadows and give a sense that this *is* the boundary.

'Principles like that, which I have explained in my writings, set very important constraints on what an architect can do. They give the limiting conditions within which one can build, but all of them are defied by modern architecture. A building can now be designed and issued as plans by somebody who is not even able to perceive it. You put the information into a computer and you rely on totally flexible materials, which will obey the computer's every whim. So, all the old principles can be safely ignored without producing an object that falls down, even if it will never stand up as we do.'

In December 2014, Scruton, along with Terry Farrell and Quinlan Terry, was appointed by British Prime Minister David Cameron to a housing design panel which, according to the Government, would 'ensure that new homes are not only lower-cost but also high-quality and well-designed, giving hardworking house buyers attractive homes that meet the demands of modern life'.[5] I ask Scruton if this was a vindication of his unwavering defence of classical architecture in the face of what he has described as 'acts of vandalism'. 'We have already submitted our report. It was very brief. The invitation came from a man in the Prime Minister's office, someone who is a classicist and who wants new houses to be designed properly – how else can we persuade the public to accept them? We had a couple of meetings and we presented our suggestions. Most impressive of all was Nicholas Boys Smith of the Create Streets organization who was and is a very strong voice. We did our best to say that there ought to be exemplars which people could follow and which embody the wisdom of classical design and the force of popular sentiment. But you are up against two major opponents: first, the architects, who don't know how to do it, and, second, the Home Builders Federation, who have profitable templates of their own. The whole idea of doing something new represents an economic loss to them.'

I ask how one might reverse forty years of bad planning to create something of the kind Scruton envisions. 'They are actually knocking down the tower blocks, but the problem is that they are not putting up anything better in the place of them. There is a question regarding what to do about the sprawling housing estates. America is full of sprawling suburbs, but they are rather charming in parts. I think what Léon Krier has done in Poundbury is a wonderful example to follow. That is to say, build the big housing estates but don't make them into housing estates. Make them into towns, with public buildings in the centre and proper streets. When a development becomes so big that people can't walk from their home to the centre, then you start another town. I think that is how it should be done.

'We need a new national consciousness of why it matters to get these things right. Supermarkets have got away with building on the edges of towns because that way they can put a car park outside the store. They can distribute food easily without the congestion of the High Street. In doing that, however, they destroy the centre of the town, since people then come to do their shopping on the edge. The High Street then dies, which is an ecological and an aesthetic disaster.

'The answer to this, if I were to give an answer, is to forbid people to build on the edge of towns. You must tell the supermarkets that they must build in the centre or be part of a shared attempt to create a new centre. That is to say, they must build in the style that is accepted in the centre, which means behind a proper façade and on a street. That means they can't get very big. Of course, they will protest, but we all have to obey laws that have an

economic cost to obeying them. For some reason people have not thought
that this principle applies to supermarkets, but it does. After all, planning
laws prevent most of us from changing our buildings in any way that we
should choose.

'I think a lot went wrong with the ascendancy of the supermarket chain
Sainsbury's. This family wormed its way into the Labour and Conservative
Parties, got sprinkled with peerages and knighthoods, and then started
investing in art – largely horrid art – and funding charities, universities
and so on. The Sainsbury name thereby became an establishment name,
and politicians felt that if you are called Sainsbury you somehow deserve
privileges that the ordinary grocer at the end of the street does not. But
nobody deserves those privileges.'

In a beautiful chapter 'Returning Home' from his memoir *Gentle Regrets*,
Scruton writes of how he and his father finally found a common cause in
their mutual repudiation of modern architecture:

> My father observed that most buildings, and most buildings that we
> truly love, are not the work of architects. The agreeable settledness of
> the old English town, he reasoned, was the work of local craftsmen,
> beings who had been lifted briefly from oblivion by Ruskin and
> Morris, but whose merely local patriotism and merely neighbourly
> ambitions had caused them to live and die unchronicled by the
> inventors of history. Architecture was, for Jack Scruton, not the cause
> of a healthy townscape but a disease of which towns must be cured.
> The true antibodies are the vernacular style, the craft tradition, the
> respect for scales and materials that had recommended themselves
> to ordinary builders in their collective attempt to settle in a home of
> their own.[6]

I ask Scruton if, through their common love of the classical vernacular,
his father finally understood him. 'This is the thing that we shared and
I greatly admired what he did in creating a movement to protect his
hometown of High Wycombe. After my mother died he went through a
period of depression, but his powers were still there and he felt a sudden

burst of freedom to use them. He married again and had the support of his second wife. So he branched out. He retired from school teaching and set up an environmental centre within the local education authority's remit. He could collect his teacher's salary while working at a little centre that children could visit. And teachers love it when they can take their pupils to a day centre and put them in the hands of someone else! The children love it too, so this renewed my father's enthusiasm for teaching and it renewed his sense that he had a mission in life. I think all this made him happier, although he was never really a happy man. And even though we found a common cause we never really got back to discussing things. The difficulties we had gone through were just too great.'

How would Scruton describe England now from an architectural perspective? 'It is, of course, a mess. At the end of the Second World War, we inherited a fairly intact environment apart from the bits that had been bombed. And the English countryside, which is a work of art in itself, has retained much of its smiling face. But wherever new building occurs, that face is very quickly wiped away. It wasn't wiped away by the old forms of building. And our old market towns as described in our nineteenth-century literature, especially by Thomas Hardy, were beautifully slotted into the countryside. They were the human habitat in a natural order. When you came across them, as I did in my youth, you would be amazed to see these little jewels, kept in place by institutions which were much more fragile than one would want them to be – institutions like the Church of England, the schools, the Women's Institute, the Scouts and all the other little platoons. Many of those towns suffered an assault from the planners and the modernist architects in the 1960s. The architects, the developers and the supermarkets saw an opportunity because our towns were not properly protected and could be pulled apart. And, sadly, many of them were. Even the ones that were bombed were more damaged by this type of development than they were by the Luftwaffe. Coventry, which was very heavily bombed and lost its cathedral, was still 60 per cent Tudor at the end of the War, but the whole lot went.'

Do children realize the great idea of England that Scruton has written about so often, especially in *England: An Elegy*? 'There are young people who respond to my book on England, but it isn't a bestseller. People are more familiar with Jeremy Paxman's facetious alternative. If you look at the History curriculum that we had when I was young, it was all about England and the kings of England, the battles, the power struggles, the constitutional changes and the colonial adventures. It was about shaping our identity. As History is taught in schools now, it consists in knowing everything about Hitler, then about Nazism, then about the Holocaust, before coming back to Hitler. And if the course touches on England at all, it will be to consider the Chartists and the Suffragettes – the movements of emancipation. The curriculum is designed to extirpate the idea of England as an object of love.'

Scruton has been a consistent defender of the British monarchy, writing in *The Meaning of Conservatism* that 'conservatives are likely to value the institution of monarchy, and the kind of patriotism that it engenders. For the legitimacy of monarchical rule arises "transcendentally", in the manner of the duties and obligations of family life. The monarch is not chosen for her personal attributes, nor does she have obligations and expectations which are the subject-matter of any "social contract". She is simply the representation of sovereignty, and its ceremonial presence. Her will as monarch is not her individual will, but the will of the state. The monarch forms part of that surface of concepts and symbols whereby citizens can perceive their social identity, and perceive society not as a means to an end, but as an end in itself. Attachment to the monarch is therefore patriotism in a pure form, a form that could not be translated into a policy, or a choice of means.'[7]

I ask him to explain, notwithstanding all the damage done to the British way of life by social egalitarianism, the lingering affection for the Royal Family. 'I would not now put it in the fulsome way I used in *The Meaning of Conservatism*. I would say rather that monarchy is natural to human beings. They want a person upon whom they can focus their emotions, and they would like that person to be above politics – occupying a permanent office that doesn't change as the political landscape changes. The Queen has fulfilled that role beautifully, but people worry that Prince Charles might not be capable of doing it and, if not, would he back out? As we know, there are legal and constitutional difficulties which caused a crisis when Edward VIII backed out in 1936, and it might cause a similar crisis again.'

If Elizabeth II has held together the old and the new England rather seamlessly, isn't there a real possibility that the whole thing will collapse when she goes? 'Put it this way: the world is in danger of collapsing at every moment! Look back to the seventeenth century and our country collapsed again and again. There was the execution of Charles I and the English thought they would never recover from that. Then there was the Long Parliament of 1640 and the total disruption of politics by Oliver Cromwell. They thought they would never recover from that, but they did. Then there was King James II: would they recover from that? They did. It was crisis after crisis, but then, by some miracle, order was established in 1688 and it went on developing in a democratic direction.'

There is also the prospect of the first celebrity king, to which Scruton quickly responds: 'We have seen it already with Princess Diana, who wanted to be a celebrity. That was her way of enjoying the position at the top. We must remember that the royal person is *not* an individual: he or she is an office, and it is very boring to be married to an office. But Diana attracted attention to herself as a celebrity and, of course, everybody identified with her. And when she died, she died a celebrity death. It was the perfect celebrity death, one actually caused by the cameras. So she became a martyr and a saint. Remember also that we have celebrity monarchs cropping up elsewhere: Spain, Holland and Sweden for example. But still people prefer to have a monarch than a president. Even hereditary presidents don't acquire the charisma of monarchy, as Bashar Assad knows to his cost.'

Does Scruton ever see a day when his country will become republican? 'Your bit of it is republican already! I can see Scotland becoming a republic, certainly. The Union is very precarious. Scotland is ruled by socialists who want revenge against England, but revenge against nothing that they can clearly define. I think this is something that, at some stage, we will have to deal with. You don't want to be governed from outside by people who don't accept your way of being. The same applies to the European Union. The political landscape is obviously going to change very radically in the next decade.'

Is Scruton sympathetic to the United Kingdom Independence Party (UKIP)? 'I am sympathetic on the great issue of migration, but I only wish the Conservative Party had made that issue *its* issue. Then it would be more like real politics. After all, UKIP doesn't have any clear policies about anything else.'

7

Why Sex?

'Obviously it's a topic that interests everyone'

In 1986, Scruton was still writing his column for *The Times* and had just published *Thinkers of the New Left*. He was fully engaged in his work in Eastern Europe. In the midst of this he published what would be, for most intellectuals, a *magnum opus*: *Sexual Desire: A Philosophical Investigation.*[1] It is a large book comprising four hundred pages and spanning the vast territory of a subject that few have dared to treat philosophically. I begin by asking Scruton how the idea of such a book came to him. 'I don't know, now that you mention it! Obviously it's a topic that interests everyone, but I suppose it goes back to having lived through the sexual revolution, and also to my experience in Italy with the dropouts from The Living Theatre. The Californian view of sex – that it is a pleasure awaiting us all and we only need liberation in order to "let it all hang out" – seemed both naïve and destructive. But I was not able to say why.

'At the same time, I had felt in myself both the bonding nature of the sexual experience, and the deep existential pain of jealousy. All of us who went through the sexual revolution had to go through those things as well. I didn't have the problems that some people had. However, I did see that liberation can only be enjoyed and exploited by a minority. It's not a great gift to offer sexual liberation to the unattractive or the helpless. That basic fact of the matter seemed to have been left out of consideration entirely, but the more I thought about it the more I realized that it went to the heart of what was wrong with the Sixties movement. I also came to the view that sexual liberation was the foundation for other ideas of liberation, all of which were equally destructive. Sex and everything associated with it is fundamental to the social order, but by making it into an individual asset that people could exploit for their own purposes, you take away from the social order the things on which we all depend. Getting sexual desire right, I felt, was the first step towards getting social reproduction right.'

Regarding the book itself, I am curious to know if it turned out as Scruton originally conceived it. 'I think it did, although it is far too long. If I wrote it now I would write it at half the length. But I did have some very strong philosophical ideas that were troubling me. In particular, I had an inkling that human beings are individuals in a manner that other objects, including animals, are not. I was working towards something that I now see as the heart of my worldview, which is that the individuality connected with the "first-person case" is something that distinguishes us completely from the rest of nature. Kant saw this, which is why I think that his philosophy gives us the truth about sexual desire even though he himself missed that truth, as he seems largely to have missed the experience too.

'Thinking about this, I wanted to press home the point – as against the Catholic worldview and more in keeping with Platonism – that the moral constraints on sexual desire don't come simply from its reproductive potential, but from the experience itself. Properly construed, sexual desire is an *interpersonal* relation, which focuses on the self-conscious subject. The moral limits on desire stem from that *metaphysical* feature.'

I remind Scruton that it was also in *Sexual Desire* that he first used concepts which would subsequently become central to his philosophical enterprise – those like *intentionality*, the *Lebenswelt* ('lived world') and the *transcendental*. He responds by telling me that 'I did actually get interested in intentionality very early on in my research. The first two things I published were on this. One was the long article "Attitudes, Beliefs and Reasons" published in 1972 in *Morality and Moral Reasoning*, which was edited by John Casey and also included essays by Simon Blackburn and Bernard Williams. I was tempted by an emotivist position in ethics back then. However, I realized that emotivism, as expressed by people like A. J. Ayer and Charles Stevenson, was totally implausible, precisely because they had overlooked the intentionality of attitudes. Attitudes and emotions are in the same order of things as beliefs. They involve a conception of an object and are responsive to reasoning. I wrote an article for *The Aristotelian Society Proceedings* on the technical side of intentionality. But as soon as I started thinking about sex, I realized that intentionality is the issue here too.

'You can describe the fundamental sexual experience as Freud does – that is, as pleasure in the sexual parts or "erogenous zones", to use his expression – but then it simply becomes a non-intentional by-product of our activity, with no essential connection with the object of desire. However, if you recognize that desire has intentionality, that it is in some measure *about* the object and not just produced by the object, and that the object is also a subject, then the whole issue changes. When I saw that, I realized that I had an interesting philosophical topic. So I looked into the literature and became quite excited by it. I was stunned by the blindness of Freud's theories and by the even more nonsensical theories of his clones and disciples such as Wilhelm Reich. In a moment of unjustified arrogance I even felt that I was unfolding the topic for the first time. The only other philosophical works that had tried to say anything about sexual desire, rather than, say, erotic love, were Sartre's *Being and Nothingness*, with its stunning apology for sado-masochism, and Aurel Kolnai's *Sexual Ethics: The Meanings and Foundations of Sexual Morality*,[2] which hadn't been translated back then. Kolnai's book was unsatisfactory because of its reliance on phenomenology, which is great as a philosophical method so long as you realize that it is trying to say something that cannot be said! And Sartre's book was unsatisfactory because it veered away from the truth, just as it was about to capture it.

'So yes, I was very intellectually stimulated while I was writing that book. I realized, for example, how Aristotle's theory of virtue could accommodate a proper theory of desire. I was able to synthesize several intellectual concerns of mine, along with my opposition to the liberationist worldview. But the essence of *Sexual Desire* is contained in the one little chapter on "The Philosophy of Love" in my more recent book *Death-Devoted Heart: Sex and the Sacred in Wagner's 'Tristan and Isolde'*.[3] This is Kant as amplified by

Hegel, and also modified by Sartre's wonderful though weird account of the attempt by the "pour-soi" to "possess the other in his freedom".

'So yes, I think *Sexual Desire* is along the right lines, but too long. Inevitably, the book upset many advocates of sexual liberation, who saw it as a kind of assault. And I didn't produce the permitted views about either homosexuality or feminism. That said, nobody reading the book now could argue that I was saying anything particularly provocative regarding those issues. I didn't entertain any hope that I would change people's perception of the subject. I just wanted to tell the truth as I saw it. It's odd that the truth as I see it seems always to annoy people, but it's not in order to annoy them that I write. It is in order to get that truth on paper, and whether that is a legitimate project can, of course, be questioned.'

I can't help enquiring if Scruton is not intentionally provocative every now and then; if he enjoys stirring up a fight? 'I wonder ... I don't think I do actually! Maybe that happens sometimes, but what always satisfied me when I finished writing something was the moment when I could say "Yes! I've got it right!" and not "Yes! They're going to hate that!"'

During our conversations, Scruton is putting the final touches to *Fools, Frauds and Firebrands*. Contemporary figures, such as French philosopher Alain Badiou and Marxist firebrand Slavoj Žižek, are given the full Scrutonian treatment. The result is a devastating analysis that leaves the reader convinced that theirs is profoundly flawed thinking. I ask Scruton if such a book is more concerned with getting to the truth than causing a stir. 'Of course. Ever since 1968, when I began reading people like Jacques Lacan and Louis Althusser, I felt that French intellectual life had been taken over by imposters. I have been very distressed by the fact that so much nonsensical literature was taken seriously *purely* because of its left-wing credentials. That was what really encouraged me to write *Thinkers of the New Left*, and, in doing so, to distinguish real thinkers like Sartre from the phonies like Althusser. And the chapter on Sartre in that book is full of praise for him, though I also point out the degradation of his political writings, the *Critique de la raison dialectique* especially.'

In the 'Epilogue' to *Sexual Desire*, Scruton takes issue with Foucault's claim that, in making sexual behaviour the object of a moral preoccupation, we 'problematise' it. He writes that what 'Foucault assumes to be an historical fact is no such thing, but rather an *a priori* truth concerning the human person. No history of thought could show the "problematisation" of sexual experience to be peculiar to certain specific social formations: it is characteristic of personal experience generally, and therefore of every genuine social order.'[4] In that book, and in both editions of *Thinkers of the New Left*, Foucault is not dismissed by Scruton as a phoney, but considered as someone who regularly displayed flashes of genius. I ask him to elaborate. 'Foucault had great literary gifts, a Ciceronian power of rhetoric and a majesty of vision which comes across even in translation. But he was also very careless of facts. The truth didn't have the same force for him as it has for you or me, and that's partly because he had a theory that truth is just the *episteme* of the ruling class. He had absorbed the *Communist Manifesto* so completely that it dictated not only his vision of human history, but his whole conception of what the intellectual life is. For him, it was about discerning powers and domination in things, and not about saying what things really *are*. Everything in Foucault's world, love and sex included, is a means to power, and nothing is an end in itself. And that, I think, is a serious intellectual defect. Put that aside, however, and you see that Foucault was a major intellect. And he could certainly write! But the extraordinary thing is that he didn't see the fraudulence of people like Althusser, Gilles Deleuze or Jacques Lacan. There's no denunciation of these imposters from him.'

When does Scruton think the corruption of French intellectual life began? 'In *Fools, Frauds and Firebrands*, I talk about the pre-history of 1968. The catastrophic defeat in the Franco-Prussian War, and then again in the First and Second World Wars, and the treasons ... When it comes to a crisis, the French suddenly realize they can't rely on each other, even denouncing their neighbours to the Gestapo. They emerged from those wars with a bad conscience and they wanted a clean sweep. Marxism offered them that clean sweep, because it aimed to rebuild society, institutions and culture from the ground up. The French intellectuals of the 1920s, especially the Surrealists, had already felt this. Most of them were on the left by then, even if there were a few dissenters like André Gide. Then Alexandre Kojève came on the scene to give the famous lectures on Hegel's *Phenomenology of Spirit* at the École des Hautes Études between 1933 and 1939.[5] All the intellectuals turned up, thinking that they'd get the answer from him. Kojève did give them an answer, and a very subtle one. He gave them Hegel's theory of "the other", as the mirror in which the self realizes its freedom. He provided them with the concepts they could use to build what was essentially an anti-national picture of the free being. The centre of social concern was henceforth not France or the Church or the family, but the self.'

Based on a report in the French newspaper *Le Monde* in 1999, it is also believed that Kojève spied for the Soviets for over thirty years. What does Scruton think of this claim? 'Whether he was an agent I simply don't know, although the French security forces say he was. But he certainly did the right thing from the point of view of Soviet strategy and he was a major architect of the European Union. Everything about him was fascinating in the same way that everything about Sartre was fascinating.

'Anyway, after the War, there was no question but that they were all going to be Marxists of some kind or another. And because the intellectual class contained geniuses like Sartre, Georges Bataille and Simone de Beauvoir, it produced not just the concepts but the individual words that people needed. In particular, it shaped the idea of the "bourgeois" – the "bourgeois" against the intellectual, against the proletarian. In this way the intellectuals could address their bad conscience about the War. The bad things the French did, they did because they were bourgeois. The good things they did, they did because they were revolutionary socialists or intellectuals, usually both.

'I think this changed everything. Of course, the French are wonderfully educated people who love books and who go on educating themselves outside universities. That is why the *café* intellectual has a huge authority with them: Sartre, de Beauvoir and Bataille all pointed in this direction. It became almost impossible for a Frenchman to think of himself as anything but a leftist devoted to the international revolution of the proletariat against the bourgeoisie. If you stood out against this, as Albert Camus did, they came down on you and annihilated you, as Sartre annihilated Camus in *Les temps modernes*.'

I remind Scruton that when people like Sartre, Foucault and Bataille were not obsessing about Marxism, they were obsessing about sex. 'Yes, of course, they were. Marxism was there in the background all the time. But they inherited from Baudelaire the ideal of the *morale du mal*, the morality of evil, which they presented as a kind of redemptive cause – witness Sartre's canonization of the thief Jean Genet. What remains to us after all the treasons of the Second World War? At least *this* remains, this posture of absolute denial. This is what grips the American professor when he comes across the literature of 1968: he encounters French intellectual life in the form of magic liturgical pronouncements. Lacan casts spells against reality, and lo! – it disappears. "There is no sexual relation!" says Lacan, and the professor falls back and says, "God, did you hear what he said: There is no sexual relation!" All Lacan is like that. "You don't ex-sist!" he declares, and his apostles exclaim, "Yea, you're right, we don't ex-sist!" Reality is just swept away and fantasy is put in the place of it. Americans try to follow the example, producing endless caricatures of the left-bank idiom, but voided of its insolence, its narcissism and its style. Everything is done so seriously and pedantically, and when the words of the French wizards are repeated in translation, without their rhetorical flourishes but simply as though they were theoretical constructs, the ridiculousness becomes apparent. But not to the American professors themselves, who fell for the trick played on them by Alan Sokal, when he submitted a po-faced satire of their idiom to the journal *Social Text* and saw it accepted for publication.

'However, I think there is another aspect of French intellectual life, which is not often noticed because it isn't spectacular in the manner of the followers of Lacan. It is straightforward, old-fashioned and scholarly, and is represented by people like Rémi Brague, Françoise Thom, Pierre Manent and Alain Besançon, who work really hard on knowing languages, studying literature and producing arguments that can be sustained. These people are highly respected in France, and are representatives of a scholarship that has always been there, though ignored by the wider world.'

When *Sexual Desire* was published in 1986, society was not, as Scruton has put it, in the 'grip of pornography'. People had not been so thoroughly reduced to their 'animal essentials'. From our perspective, the world seemed so much more innocent. I ask him if he thinks there is any way back from the 'pornofied' society in which we now live. 'You never know whether there's a way back. Consider Aldous Huxley's *Brave New World*: is there a way back from it? Of course, there isn't! When it has got to that point, the only thing the savage can do is hang himself. If there is a way back, it has first to come through people's consciousness that their condition is unsustainable. If, as I hope, a general awareness dawns that the emerging society is not just trapped in a condition of lovelessness, but also unable to reproduce itself, there will be a collective revulsion, and maybe even the decision to turn back. One cannot hope for anything else.

'However, human nature may not permit this; there may not be the movement of revulsion that will cause people to change course. In which case, people will stop reproducing. One always hopes that a conversion experience will occur, or that a crucial relationship will change everything. In my novel *The Disappeared*,[6] the character Yunus is somebody who lives with a thoroughly divided and divisive view of sex: there are the unknowable, untouchable women watching him from behind their veils; and there are the knowable, bruisable women who are mere objects, so many yards of female flesh. He is divided because he has to maintain the image of feminine purity, embodied in his sister, a person who must never be polluted. But then, this extraordinary thing happens to him: he encounters Laura, and in the moment of trying to rape her is forced to think about her in the way he thinks about his sister. And then everything changes, and it changes through love. I think that scenario is perfectly plausible, and it is the turning point of the narrative. It is what enables all of the characters, save two, to be rescued in the end.'

In a lecture at McGill University in Montreal in 2014, Scruton offered an appendix to his book *The Soul of the World*,[7] in which he argued the 'self-conscious experience of sex as a "going out" towards the other presupposes transcendental categories: the sacred, the redemptive, the innocent, the pure and the polluted. It is not enough to think of our sexual relations merely in contractual terms, as though the only relevant question from the moral perspective is the question of consent. For offences against innocence, decency, purity and the sanctity of the other can be as well inflicted by consent as by coercion. To describe these wrongs we must make use of transcendental categories … Moreover, if we do not use these concepts, or other concepts from the same family ... we will relate to each other as objects, not subjects, and to that extent fail to relate.'[8] I ask Scruton to pursue this crucial idea. 'There is an emerging human type which doesn't take risks, which doesn't go out to the other and which doesn't form attachments on account of never having been attached as a child. I have a kind of dystopian vision of what this might mean in the long run. I envisage a society of reduced humans, who are just bodies, like the sad products of the Romanian orphanages. And while, from time to time, a child may be created, as a random by-product of their sexual pleasures, it will be left on the doorstep of the state, so ensuring that it too will grow up as a stranger in a world of the estranged.'

What, if anything, can conscientious parents do to protect their children from this debased idea of human sexuality? 'Obviously, the traditional way was through religion. Nowadays, parents try to shift the obligation onto teachers, and then teachers think the children should have classes on sex education. The classes then get infected by the very same disease, since the self-appointed experts are only there because they have lost sight of what matters in sex, which is the part that must be hidden. To be honest, I don't know what the answer is. I think each person has to confront it for himself. Going back to the themes of *The Disappeared*, the education of the Muslim girl in this country largely involves keeping her away from the surrounding society. Through that practice, Muslim boys understand that the sexual relation depends on chastity and virginity in the woman, if it is to be successful. But the society surrounding them is not like that, so they get the idea that you can exploit it. The result is crimes of the kind that shocked us when their extent was revealed in Rotherham, where whole neighbourhoods were infected by the view that indigenous girls are really whores to be exploited. Their purity has been lost and once lost is lost forever.

'That particular way of reacting to the sexual revolution is extreme and the result of ways of thinking that we had wrongly supposed would never be seen in modern Western societies. But it is also a consequence of the sensual and pleasure-grabbing view of sex that has invaded the modern way of seeing human relations. I really do worry about this, but at least the schools which my children attend seem to be pretty good at marginalizing the sexual culture. One hopes that sex will be, for them, inseparable from love, and not the degraded thing that is marketed on the Internet.'

Of course, this new sexually permissive society is not free from moralistic edicts about how a person should speak or what he can and cannot eat. Scruton has often referred to this fact, writing in *I Drink Therefore I Am* that 'what is most interesting to the anthropologist is the ease with which puritan outrage can be displaced from one topic to another, and the equal ease with which the thing formerly disapproved of can be overnight exonerated from all taint of sin.'[9] 'This is,' he tells me, 'an extraordinary phenomenon. We've observed that Puritanism transfers itself from the thing where it is at home, which is the life of the spirit, to the thing where it is alien and counterproductive, which is the life of the body. Parliament votes with hardly any opposition, and no discussion, for the proposal that cigarettes must now be sold in plain packets. This will produce a devastating claim in damages, and do nothing to reduce the number of smokers; but nobody seems to care because it is a way of punishing sin, the only sin that now matters, which is the sin against the body. At the same time nothing is said about Internet pornography, its addictive consequences and the day-by-day wreckage of the human soul that results from it. That is how displacement mechanisms work – by attracting attention away from what is serious and alarming, to what is trivial and easy to attack.

'The health fascists adopt a materialist view of the human being. Their view is that we don't look after the souls of human beings, but we do look after their bodies because their bodies are the concern of the Welfare State and a cost to the taxpayer. The only sin that you can commit is the sin against your own body, and you do this by taking the wrong substances. But even then, if it's seen under the aspect of "liberation", it doesn't matter what you take. And so, in America, campaigns to permit the smoking of cannabis are conducted by the very people who are also campaigning against the tobacco industry! The smoking of cannabis is not just risky in the way that smoking tobacco is risky, but it also has a seriously negative neurological effect. It is destructive not just to the person who smokes but to everyone around him, because it undermines his ability to relate to others in a responsible way. The British scientist Baroness Susan Greenfield has been saying this for some years, but I think she's in a state of despair because nobody wants to listen. And this, despite the fact that cannabis is probably the most dangerous thing you can take, apt to precipitate irreversible psychosis in the vulnerable.'

In the final chapter of *Sexual Desire*, Scruton introduced the concept of the *sacred* for the first time in his writings. What would become a centrepiece of his later work was employed to emphasize the importance of marriage as a human ceremony which 'marks the transition from one state of existence to another. At such moments, man is confronted with his fragility and dependence. As at the moments of birth and death, he is beset by awe. This feeling is a recognition of the sacred, of the intrusion into the human world of obligations that cannot be created by an act of choice, and which therefore demand a transcendental meaning. The sacred is "the subjectivity of objects" – the presentation, in the contours of day-to-day things, of a meaning that sees "from I to I". Out of the mute objectivity of the surrounding world, a voice suddenly calls to me, with a clear and intelligible command. It tells me who I am, and enjoins me to enter the place that has been kept for me.'[10]

I enquire if, while writing *Sexual Desire*, he envisioned how this concept of the sacred would function in his subsequent work. 'Yes, I had an inkling of what I was going to go on to think. I have been very influenced in all this by Wagner, and in particular by the way in which he tries to rescue the sexual bond from the rest of nature as a thing apart. Even if there are no gods to endow it with its special nature, desire attracts to itself an aura of existential risk: it is a point of transition, a liminal experience, where we tread in trepidation on the inner life of another. That is the kind of experience from which ideas of the sacred and the desecrated arise. I think that it is Wagner's great contribution to our understanding of sexuality, and our understanding of human life more generally, to have perceived this and dramatized it. The sacred is something that erupts of its own accord in our experience. But it is also true that, for many people, this eruption never happens. The sexual bond, even if it has these moments of transcendence, isn't sufficiently strong to sustain us for a lifetime. It asks to be fed into and supported by a *religious structure* – a structure that makes repetition meaningful. That is the fundamental purpose of liturgy. Marriage is part of religion and develops out of it. Even if it hasn't been declared a sacrament, marriage must be understood as a vow, not a contract, a mutual self-giving which calls on the gods to bear witness and to give effect to it.'

Finally, does Scruton see a link between the loss of the old sexual virtues and the rise of the philosophy of animal rights? 'If we think that we are just animals, then it's very difficult to make the distinction between the rules that govern our behaviour to each other, and the rules that govern our behaviour to other animals. Interestingly enough, however, the sentimentality about animals can go with total coldness towards people, as with Hitler. Animals are easy to relate to because they don't make moral judgements, and that is why they don't have rights either. You can only have rights if you have duties, and animals live a life that is, so to speak, duty-free. This does not mean that we can treat animals as we wish: moral beings have duties of compassion and mutual aid that stretch far beyond the sphere of rights.

'People need to relate to the natural environment, and in our overpopulated world it is very difficult to come across an animal in its natural condition. You only come across pets and domestic animals, or creatures that you regard as plagues, such as mice and rats. So the idea that we exist in a natural hierarchy of animals has been eroded. We welcome animals into our lives as fellow beneficiaries of the Welfare State. The family dog inevitably becomes a passive object of affection, and people increasingly build their morality around that relationship. It then becomes difficult to exclude things that look like dogs – foxes, badgers and so on. Most draw the line at rats; but very few wish to follow their sentiments through to the conclusion drawn by some Hindus, which is that nothing in the world is more sacred than a cow. Concerning our relations to other forms of life, a vast confusion reigns, and I have tried to address that confusion in some of my writings, notably in *Animal Rights and Wrongs*.'

8

Leaving Birkbeck for Boston

'*Everything in me was tending in a single direction*'

In 1992, Roger Scruton decided to leave Birkbeck College after a period of twenty years. He was a full professor with his own chair and all the entitlements that went with it. So why did he opt to forgo the status and security of the academic establishment? 'Life in the university was not so easy in the 1980s. I was targeted by the Socialist Workers Party as a "fascist". The principal cause was the Honeyford affair, although *The Salisbury Review* didn't help and *Thinkers of the New Left* only confirmed the prevailing suspicions. At a certain stage, I wrote a *Times* article on a man named Patrick Harrington, who was discovered by his fellow students at North London Polytechnic to be a member of the National Front.[1] Essentially, they had intimidated him and tried to exclude him from lectures. So I wrote an article pointing out that the "the interesting thing is that these professed opponents of discrimination and brutality have used every available measure of intimidation in order to ruin the career of a fellow student, while the 'Nazi agitator' [Harrington], instead of summoning his storm-troopers to the rescue, has merely petitioned the courts. One does not have to be a National Front sympathizer to wonder who, in this encounter, is the 'fascist'".'

'Harrington then applied for a postgraduate course at Birkbeck, for which we normally required a second-class honours grade one (2:1) as a minimum. I happened to be external examiner in philosophy at North London Polytechnic at the time, though all examining was anonymous and so I had no knowledge of Harrington's likely result. In any case my colleagues at Birkbeck reacted with alarm, crying "Oh no, we can't have him!" I disagreed, saying that we can't repeat the injustice that has been done to him at his previous institution, and we must judge the case on its merits. So let's see if he gets a 2:1. If he doesn't, then of course he won't get in. To my great relief, he got a 2:2. So the case was dropped and I thought that was the end of it. But then there appeared a little gossip column in the *Observer*, which talked about Harrington as a fascist member of the student body at North London Polytechnic and candidate for an MA at Birkbeck who, despite the enthusiastic support of that well-known right-wing red-haired guru Roger Scruton, was not admitted. The damaging implication was that I had abused my position to promote a fellow fascist, despite his lack of qualifications. I insisted on an apology and the paper refused. I therefore had to sue.

'During the court case, the journalist who wrote the gossip column said that he was simply reporting sources within the college. Maybe there was a colleague who had said those damaging things, though I doubt it. Anyway, the *Observer* lost the case and I won damages of £75,000, which was, for me, a very large sum. Maybe, with such a sum in the bank I could go out into the real world. After all, I was not happy at Birkbeck; my friends were in journalistic, literary and political circles. I had been divorced for a long time and had not remarried. I had no dependants. I had other sources of income, such as my journalism and a conveyancing business that I had set up with a student of ours at Birkbeck who was also a surveyor. My energies were also involved in Eastern Europe.'

What of the precise circumstances surrounding Scruton's departure from Birkbeck? 'I was owed some sabbatical and so I took a year's leave in 1990, which was extremely advantageous because that was just after the Berlin Wall had come down and my help was needed in Czechoslovakia. I was able to go over to Brno for a few months and do some work in setting things up. It was a lonely, bleak time because everyone was so disoriented. Of course, they were glad about the fall of communism, but they didn't know where they were going. I had already sold my flat in Notting Hill Gate, and when I returned from Brno went to live in a little cottage in Stanton Fitzwarren, outside Swindon, which I rented from the Moonies – a story I tell in *On Hunting*. I also had a little room that I rented from Alan Clark in Albany in London.

'During the last years of communism, when our various trusts had depended on a developed messenger service, I had used three young men – graduate students who had attached themselves to me – to travel in Eastern Europe. They were extremely keen to take advantage of the new situation. Western investors needed contacts in government, in the press and in the legislature, in order to lobby on behalf of their interests. We knew the new elite, the people in government and those who had come up from underground – many of them were personal protégés of mine. The big government relations consultancies were in the habit of dealing only with communists – the Gorbachev types, with whom, as Mrs Thatcher famously (and ignorantly) said, you can do business. So they were, briefly, on the back foot, which gave us time to seize a little bit of the market. The Czech and Hungarian branches of our venture didn't do very well. But the Polish branch was in time amazingly successful thanks to the energy and commitment of Marek Matraszek. I quickly realized that I should get out of it, since I saw those countries in another light from that of business. But for a brief period the three boys paid me for the benefit of my advice. This encouraged me to think that I could leave the university and live as a consultant.

'Then I was offered a part-time job at Boston University by the then president John Silber. Although a Democrat who came second in the race to become governor of Massachusetts in 1990, Silber was also a Kant scholar with a very old-fashioned view about education, which he had found endorsed in some of my writings. The title of "university professor" was then in the gift of the President of the University, so that it could be offered even to a class traitor and an enemy of the people. I insisted that the position be part-time, however, because I wanted to write.

'My one-semester job left me free from teaching for eight months of the year. And as a university professor I didn't have examining duties. I taught a graduate course at Boston on the philosophy of music and this formed the basis of my book *The Aesthetics of Music*.[2] The rest of the job was not so easy as I had hoped. I had to teach a course in elementary philosophy which was attended by over a hundred students, some of whom couldn't yet speak English. And because I was used to the British tutorial system I felt obliged to look at all their essays and to give individual supervisions on how to improve them – which meant, sometimes, on how to write an English sentence with a full stop at the end. Although this part of the job was strenuous and exhausting, it allowed me to develop a series of lectures that I first gave at Birkbeck and which eventually became *Modern Philosophy: An Introduction and Survey*.[3] It also introduced me to some highly intelligent and interesting students, two of whom – Joanna Binkowski and Lydia Moland – became lifelong friends.'

Before moving to Boston, had Scruton ever considered writing a comprehensive book on music? 'I had always wanted to do for music what I had tried to do for architecture. *The Aesthetics of Music*, like *The Aesthetics of Architecture*, starts from first principles, from the very basic metaphysical question of what a sound is. That question is hardly ever discussed in the literature, but I wanted to start from what was fundamental and then work towards a theory of the place of music in culture as a whole. It was, however, a great shock for me to discover that, even at graduate level, there were areas of American students' minds that had never been cultivated at all. The first example I introduced to the class was the piece of music that had got me thinking about counterpoint and sonata form all those years before: Mendelssohn's *Hebrides Overture*. Only two of the students of the thirty present had ever heard it! And then I came to learn that some of them had heard nothing except AC/DC and U2. That was a real education for me, because it meant that I had to start listening to rock, metal and pop in order to form an opinion about them. But it was also an education for the students because, in listening to the musical examples I played, many of them had a great awakening. That was very gratifying!'

I ask Scruton to elaborate on the central distinctions, as he perceived them, between the British system of university education and that which he experienced at Boston. 'The most important structural distinction between

British and American universities is that, in American universities, the professor is both the teacher and the examiner of the student. He assigns a grade to the student on what he, the professor, has taught and nobody tells the professor what he *should* teach. The professor is essentially awarding grades to himself. So, there are huge possibilities of corruption, and people often make no effort to avoid them, giving an A to everyone, for example, or penalizing students who do not agree with their views. In the British system there is an independent curriculum, which is validated by people outside the university and anonymously examined by those who haven't necessarily taught the students concerned. In other words, there is an attempt, even in the humanities, to create a system of objective knowledge, which is examined by people other than those who have taught it. That, of course, is how it should be. If it works at all, the American system does so despite lacking this feature. It works when there is a teacher who really can teach, who really does know the subject and who really is impartial when grading. That is a rare thing. On the other hand at Boston there were, and are, some truly great teachers; something that the system encourages because the students have nothing else on which to depend, so that they egg their professors on to realize *their* potential. One such teacher, the cultural historian Jim Johnson, became a good friend and married Lydia Moland, whom I mentioned earlier. They have been among my closest friends ever since.

'In philosophy, America has produced some very powerful figures, such as Saul Kripke, Donald Davidson, Willard Van Orman Quine and Hilary Putnam – people who could see through a problem and respond with a vision. I had the good fortune on my first visit to America in 1979 to attend Kripke's lectures on identity at Princeton. It was my first encounter with genius, and it illustrated the openness of the American system, which permits such things to emerge and reveal themselves. This compensates greatly for the possibilities of corruption and the constant collapse of standards. However it also depends on an atmosphere of cooperation between intelligent students and ambitious professors, all of whom are seeking to shine. You find that atmosphere in Princeton, but by no means everywhere else.

'American philosophy is therefore marked by an outgoing, didactic spirit that has no real equivalent in Britain. The original pragmatists like William James and C. S. Peirce were important literary figures. They wanted a philosophy that engaged with the culture, and in William James they had a writer as great as any that philosophy has produced, almost as great as his brother Henry. The pragmatists absorbed the technical approach to philosophy that grew out of the logic of Frege and Russell, and which was brought to America by the Central European exiles – by Carnap, Neurath and von Neumann, among others. The synthesis of pragmatism and formal logic was effected by Quine, whose elegance of style was accompanied by an extreme succinctness and vividness of thought. In his works you encounter a distinctive shining of the American genius: his writing is at one and the same time abstract in conception and concrete in style.

'Pragmatism was later identified with Richard Rorty and made into another kind of relativism. John Dewey, whom Rorty cited as his principal inspiration, was a really damaging figure in American culture. Although he had some important things to say, he was not great in the way that Peirce and James were great. He was what Schopenhauer would have called an unscrupulous optimist – a bland, bigoted, good-natured character who showed how bad a good nature can be, with its hare-brained schemes for the reform of everything and self-complacent belief in its own impeccable virtue. It is thanks to Dewey that our departments of education espoused the "child-centred" approach to teaching and learning, which effectively expelled knowledge and discipline from the classroom. It should be said that Rorty was first-rate before he fell under the spell of Dewey and pragmatism. He had a very strange conversion experience, a conversion from something to nothing. But there you are!'

I can't leave American philosophy without asking Scruton about Noam Chomsky, of whom he once wrote: 'Chomsky's political thinking is too devoid of theory for my purposes – and indeed little better than a pose, although a pose furiously adhered to.'[4] If Scruton were to sum Chomsky up, what would he say? 'There are really two people there: the linguistician who had important and original ideas, even if the best of his ideas are incipient in Frege and Tarski. Chomsky developed those ideas in the context of evolutionary theory, thus putting the subject of psycho-linguistics on the map. And nobody in his right mind would dismiss his achievement, or the sharp intelligence that gave rise to it.

'However, there is also the public persona, who is completely independent of the linguistician. As I see it, this other person is a spoilt brat in the American mould, sounding off against Daddy, one who has had everything, feels guilty and wants to find a victim to identify with and through whom to purify his soul. He goes on making trouble for comfortable people on those grounds, using his intellect in order to prove that he's always one stage higher than his opponent. Of course, he has no judgement, supporting whatever cause happens to be irritating to the American body-politic. And he pretends to himself, and not just to the world, that his favoured causes are not despotic until finally (as with the Khmer Rouge) he has to admit that they are. Sartre, of course, was the same about Vietnam. He was finally forced to confront the truth when thousands of Vietnamese refugees started arriving in Paris. Chomsky, however, was not taken in by the Parisian nonsense machine and has done a very good job of demolishing Lacan and his circle, as you can discover on the web.'

After only three years, Scruton left Boston in 1995. Why did he leave and was he tempted to stay? 'By then I had worked out that I could leave because I had enough money from other sources and I had also bought this farm. My heart was here along with all my projects. I had failed to put down any roots over there, and America is a very lonely place if you have no family to shield yourself from the emptiness. There is no university life in America because your colleagues live out in the suburbs and drive twenty miles back and forth at the beginning and end of each day. Their lives are pure, hygienic, and they return to their 2.5 children from the office with a sense of the perennial blessedness of the suburbs, where you can be alone with your family among people who are alone in just the same way. Therefore suddenly, at five o'clock, all the classrooms are empty and everything is deserted. I confronted desolation at the end of each day, and a great existential question haunted those empty classrooms, asking "why am I here?" I trudged home to my lonely place and fought off the urge for a solitary cocktail.

'Those who settle in American universities usually go there with their families. They take advantage of the schools, pensions and so on. But at the time I had no interest in such things. None of this prevented me from attempting to settle in America later, of course, when I too had a family.'

I recall Scruton once saying that, each weekend, he would fly home from Boston to hunt. When I mention this, he smiles and remarks that 'in those days, you could get on an aeroplane and fly home very cheaply. I was determined to hunt, so it was a thrill to be able to come home and master the art of it.' And moving to the country, how did that come about? 'I found Sunday Hill Farm through a relocation agent who was also a hunt follower and who lived around the corner in a little farm of his own. I said to him that I'd like to live down here permanently and keep a horse at home, and one day he came up with a place that had come on the market. The woman who owned it wanted to get out as quickly as possible. Her life had gone wrong and the man responsible had left. The place was a sheep farm of twenty-nine acres, totally run down. I came to look at it in the autumn with Christina, who danced joyfully across the meadows, and remarked that there was grass *pour une centaine de chevaux*. The owner was sitting before the cast iron stove with a Jane Austen novel in her lap. Around her were gallon-jars of plum juice, fermenting into wine. She had not recovered from the wild gamekeeper with whom she had fled, Lady Chatterley-like, to this place, and now wanted to flee again with her daughter, leaving everything behind, including the carpets that smelled of cats and the fields littered with broken wire and dead machinery. The house was very small and had been neglected, so it would be a task to get it right. But the owner didn't want to put it in the hands of an agent. She refused to have a survey, just as she was now clearly determined to keep all her memories to herself, tightly packed and unexamined. She told us that she would accept the best price, that we could put in bids on a certain day, but that she would not accept anything less than £175,000. Paul Greenwood, the relocation agent, said to me that if the others know that, they will offer £180,000. And somebody thinking that will offer £181,000, so you have to offer £181,250. So I did and I got it! It's worth ten times that now, of course, and I have added land to it. It is up from twenty-nine acres to one hundred and five.'

And so, after twenty-three years, Scruton left academic life and found himself on Sunday Hill Farm. But was hunting really the catalyst that finally pulled him away from all that he knew to live here in the country? 'Yes, hunting was *the* crucial thing. I didn't fit into the university – that had been established. Neither did I particularly like the American university. I could live independently through journalism and the East European consultancy business and there would be other business opportunities, I was sure. Thanks to winning the libel action to which I referred earlier, I was able to buy this farm without a mortgage and I didn't have any debts. Money was coming in one way or another and I didn't have very many commitments.'

How did this transition to country life change Scruton's daily routine? 'Anyone who has had the experience of a job in the city, and who has then moved to the country to find himself in the middle of nature, will be exhilarated at first. You feel privileged, let off like a child out of school. For a long while I just rejoiced in that fact. But then came the question of justifying this joy. So I was always giving myself tasks. By that time, I had so settled into writing as my profession that it really didn't change very much. Wherever I am, I can get up and go to a desk and start writing, and that was true then too.'

Scruton's first major publication of the 1990s was *The Philosopher on Dover Beach*, a broad-ranging book that encompassed subjects as diverse as Hegel, Picasso and George Bernard Shaw. Some of the essays were reviews, others were drawn from Scruton's contributions to *The Salisbury Review*, and there were some recently published pieces, including 'Man's Second Disobedience'. It was also obvious that Scruton's writing style was beginning to take a unique shape, and that his philosophical vision of the human person had come to fruition. In a vein that would become distinctly Scrutonian, he writes that there

is an attitude that we direct to the human person, and which leads us to see, in the human form, a perspective on the world that reaches from a point outside it. We may direct this very attitude, on occasion, to the whole of nature, and in particular to those places, things, events and artefacts where freedom has been real. The experience of the sacred is the sudden encounter with freedom; it is the recognition of personality and purposefulness in that which contains no human will.[5]

Does Scruton agree that this book offered the first glimpse at what would become his worldview? 'Yes, that is entirely true. The ten years of the Eighties had been very formative for me, because those were the years when I worked in Eastern Europe on the communist problem. I also had my column in *The Times* and was editing *The Salisbury Review*. Everything in me was tending in a single direction, which was to articulate an experience that was transformative in itself, and to give voice to my worldview. And the style came out of that.'

I put it to Scruton that in *The Philosopher on Dover Beach* Kant's moral theory takes on a quasi-religious dimension, as when he writes:

Kant's theory of freedom shows us how we might understand the sacred and the miraculous. Our understanding of the miraculous is like our understanding of the person. When we see another's smile we see human flesh moving in obedience to impulses in the nerves. No law of nature is suspended in this process: we smile not in spite of, but because of, nature. Nevertheless, we understand a smile in quite another way: not as flesh, but as spirit, freely revealed. A smile is always more than flesh for us, even if it is only flesh.[6]

He responds: 'Yes, definitely. I suppose that was a slow recognition of truths which had been dawning on me in the book on sexual desire, and which had never been totally out of my mind anyway. But the truths that were dawning in *Sexual Desire* took a new form, because they were detached now from the specific experience of the sexual and were made more fundamental to our social being as such. *The Philosopher on Dover Beach* contains essays that are important in that regard, and many of the ideas expressed there became internalized into my thinking. The arguments about Hegel, corporate personality and aesthetics are all important to me. Finally, however, the most significant of the essays for me was "Man's Second Disobedience: Reflections on the French Revolution". That crystallized my thoughts about what had happened in that great event, and also rationalized what I had felt in 1968 in Paris.'

If *The Philosopher on Dover Beach* would set the scene for much of Scruton's subsequent writings, it was clear that his new life in the country also had a profound effect on the way he wrote and perceived the world. As we have seen, central to that life was hunting and central to hunting, as Scruton tells me, 'is the experience of reconnection: I am being connected to something bigger than myself, which is not just a particular human community and its way of life, but also the animal world – to my "species being" as Ludwig Feuerbach would say. I am no longer maintaining my position in the world simply through intellectual work, but I am being maintained by my membership of something else. That, I think, has been very important – those beside me are people that I know and we are doing this together. We haven't got much in common, any more than I have much in common with the horses and the hounds. But we do have *this* in common, and it is much more deeply implanted in our nature as hunter-gatherers than my work on Hegel. Reconnecting to something primordial is a release of something that had for too long been imprisoned within.

'To be part of a collective enterprise in which three species are giving each other support: *that* is a most extraordinary thing. The ceremony too, like military parades and the changing of the guards, represents something far deeper than the business of the moment. Institutions without ceremony have a tawdry, improvised air to them. They're just like firms or bureaucracies. A ceremony is a way of acknowledging the existence of others, not others alive only, but others dead and unborn. It is through ceremony that you appeal to the observer, the stranger, to the person who wants to know what's going on. You are trying to stand up and vindicate yourself, to be proud of yourself as a member of something greater than yourself. So people are recognized in ceremonies for what they really are, which is what they are *for others*. It is a tragedy that ceremony is disappearing from our world. In my book *On Hunting* I quote Yeats's famous line: "How but in custom and in ceremony are innocence and beauty born?" It is only a rhetorical question, but it is a very powerful question. Beauty and innocence are disappearing, and that has something to do with the loss of formalities generally.

'Those formalities went out of fashion at Oxford and Cambridge after the Sixties. The attitude was: we don't wear suits; we don't wear academic gowns; we won't dine in hall; we go out for a burger. And hall, especially in lefty places like Balliol, was made into something totally informal. The students themselves have now rebelled against this. In most colleges, they have asked for proper formal hall at least twice a week, so that they can dress properly, wear their gowns and be something other than the slobs they were.'

Shortly after leaving Boston in 1995, Scruton published *Animal Rights and Wrongs*, a book that took a stance opposed to the animal rights campaigners.[7] 'Public discussion', he wrote in the text's preface, 'has become ever more confused. In my view the confusion has a metaphysical cause. People lack the concepts that would enable them to understand the deep differences between animals and humans. The old ideas of the soul, free-will and eternal judgement, which made the distinction between people and animals so important and so clear, have lost their authority, and nothing adequate has come in place of them. Creatures were once divided into those with a rational soul and those without one. Now the division is between pets and pests, distinguished not by their habits, but by their appearance. Pets are granted honorary status of the human community, itself Disneyfied to include them ... It goes without saying that this division between the pet and the pest has no basis in reality.'[8]

I ask Scruton if he would have written such a book had he not found hunting. 'No. As a matter of fact, I wrote that book at the time when, growing out of the Eastern European business to which I referred earlier, Sophie and I had established a media relations consultancy here in England, so as to give advice on crafting and delivering messages. The Countryside Alliance was our first client. All attempts to explain hunting to the journalists, or to get a balanced discussion in the media or in Parliament, were frustrated by the fact that deep philosophical questions were constantly being fudged or ignored for the sake of emotion. It seemed to me that something was needed that addressed the animal rights question from first principles, and not in the question-begging way of Peter Singer.[9] If it was written in the right way then maybe journalists would be able to draw on it, when setting up their "for and against" debating points. I discussed the matter with Geoff Mulgan, who was an adviser to Tony Blair and was just setting up Demos, and he said this is exactly the type of subject we would like to cover. By then, of course, I was already involved in hunting and seriously interested in the general argument about our relations to other species – something that has occupied much of my writing since. I felt the argument to be singing in me as I wrote the book, and how depressing it was to see that it had no effect!

'The Kantianism in my book on sexual desire re-emerges in the book on animals. I am appealing to the same vision of the human person. I recognize, however, that there is something deep within our nature that requires us to anthropomorphize animals. By doing so, we adapt to the species among which we live. Linguists recognize species-identification as one of the first capacities to express itself in the learning of language – that is, an ability to recognize that *this* and *this* belong to the same species even though they look completely different, whereas *this* and *this* don't, even though they look the same. That capacity seems to be deep in the human being and you can see why it is an adaptation. So it emerges very quickly, especially in children's stories, that animals have a species character, and they are anthropomorphized accordingly.

'It is also true that every society and culture that we know of, from the beginning of recorded history, has stories regarding anthropomorphized animals. Aesop's fables, for example, would be directed often at children. You learn about yourself in this way and it's not necessarily sentimental. The old stories of animals showed them in their natural condition: foxes tear the geese apart, wolves attack the flock and lions kill men. It is only in recent times that anthropomorphism has been taken one stage further, so as to deprive animals of their animality and to endow them with a caricature of the human soul. You can do that, of course, with cartoons and animations on the screen. I think this has taken things in a completely new direction. People are sentimental about animals because animals can do no wrong; but they can do no wrong because they can do no right.'

Scruton campaigned vigorously against the hunting ban in England, instituted by Tony Blair's government in 2004. I ask him if the ban was an abject failure. 'Not an abject failure, since people still go out hunting and foxes are still pursued – but not, of course, in the same way. People now lay a trail, but the hounds don't necessarily follow that trail. They'll follow the scent of a fox and the temptation is to turn a blind eye to what they are doing. The problem is that the law forbids hunting without defining it. So we don't actually know what has been forbidden by the Act. It is a huge thing in English law to create a new crime. The Common Law hates that! And the reason why there is no definition of hunting in the Act is that those who made the law knew nothing about it. They didn't know, for example, that the people on horseback are not part of the action: they are following the hounds, and they don't particularly care what the hounds are doing so long as they can see them and enjoy the chase. And the huntsman is not himself hunting the fox: he is "hunting hounds", as it is called. So then we must ask: who is hunting what? Until you define that, the law is empty. Moreover, you cannot outlaw an activity on which a community depends without inviting that community to find ways round the law. Imagine what would happen if there were a law passed against football!'

Scruton shows me an article that he has just published in *Wiltshire Life*, his local magazine, elaborating the point:

> The opponents of hunting seldom perceive that it is an activity around which people build their lives, as I have built mine. Of course hunting has had to change as a result of recent legislation. But in one form or another it will continue, since apart from its vital function in managing wildlife it is one of the ways in which the attachment between people and their landscape is renewed.
>
> Looking from my window on this summer day I see the fields that it is my duty to maintain as an agricultural resource. I see rye-grass planted for silage, hedges laid to contain cattle and to keep out my neighbour's sheep, and a fenced-off corner for pigs. I worry about the docks and the thistles; I am troubled by the muck-heap and wonder whether we shall be able to spread it before the autumn. I see a gap in the hedge where the sheep could get through, and a broken culvert in the ditch which could block up in the winter rains. Those thoughts are the premises of husbandry, and they depend on distinguishing my rights and duties from the rights and duties of my neighbour.

But I also see a covert planted as habitat, a tiger-trap across a ditch, a hunt jump in the hedgerow and a headland set aside for horses to pass. I worry that the tiger-trap is rotten, that the hedge is now too tall to jump, that the fields are inadequately drained and will become impassable. Those thoughts are no longer part of husbandry, and depend on no division between 'mine' and 'thine'. This sense of common ownership and common destiny is part of what turns the land into a landscape. The fields that I see from my window do not end at my boundary but stretch beyond it, to the place where the hounds of the VWH must be called off from the territory of the Old Berkshire, where 'ours' becomes 'theirs', and the riot of followers must turn at last for home.

That feeling of 'ours' is expressed in many social events besides hunting: in fun rides, farmers' breakfasts, hunt balls, the pony club and point-to-points. Those events form part of an intricate web of social relations through which we join in the collective possession of our whole locality, and override our separate private claims. The 'we' feeling of the hunt is the prime reason why our boundaries are so meticulously maintained, and also so elaborately punctured. It is the cause of coverts and copses and ponds, and also the reason why many originally urban people like myself are prepared to invest their money in a landscape that the farmers themselves are struggling now to maintain.

This sense of belonging without owning is not something recent. But, such is the heat of political passion that hunting inspires in those who have never engaged in it, that the feeling is rarely understood for what it is – a root cause of the English landscape. Of no landscape is that more true than the stretch of North Wiltshire where I have the great good fortune to live.

As a man who is now in his seventies, does Scruton see any danger in hunting at his age? 'Yes, but it is not as dangerous as many of the things one does, such as driving a car to Swindon.'

9

Farming and Family

'*I am not a heroic person*'

For more than twenty years, Roger Scruton has divided his time between writing and farming. But was it easy for him to adapt to his new farming life? 'It wasn't hard because I had already been renting a country cottage and going down at weekends, and my whole desire was to move permanently to the country. I wanted to shake off the academic world. I wanted to take seriously my calling as a writer. That said, it is not as though I live miles away from London: it is perfectly feasible to live here and appear there when needed. The only concern has been loneliness, because it is much harder to form a circle of sympathetic friends in the country. You can belong to the little platoons, in the way I described in connection with hunting. You can be on good or bad terms with the neighbours, but to find someone who would sing through the Schubert *Lieder* while you play the piano – well, as you can imagine, I have not succeeded at that! Accompanying a singer has been one of my most important forms of relaxation and I have been deprived of it ever since moving to this place.'

In reading Scruton, you get the feeling that farming was a sort of coming home, a feeling that he was always meant to be here. Is that true? 'I wouldn't say it was a coming home, because I was not brought up in the country. As I tell it in *News from Somewhere*, mine is essentially a story of a nowhere person arriving somewhere, and trying to bring with him the economic life that will rescue that somewhere for a few more years. In this neighbourhood, I am the first person in recent times to have employed anyone outside the immediate family. Our neighbours cannot afford to employ other people, and even if they could, they would be mad to do so, since modern employment law makes an employee a far closer dependant than a wife or a child. So I was aware from the beginning that I'm not really here on the terms the place itself creates. I am here on my own terms and depend on a financial backing without which I could not possibly settle down far from the city.'

Does he have a philosophy of farming? 'Actually, I do. I have no doubt that the transition from hunter-gatherer to farmer was the greatest of all transitions our species has undergone. It involves changing our relation to our environment completely. The hunter-gatherer is supported by the environment; the farmer supports it. We have re-made the relation between man and nature as one of mutual dependence. So if farming is to be done properly, it must also be a nurturing and a tending of the land, a kind of *stewardship*. That is the premise from which any agricultural philosophy should begin, and it is a premise that is ignored by most modern agribusiness. Settling here I became quite environmentally conscious and, in my own little way, an eco-freak – but not one who is aggressively disposed to attack the modern agricultural economy in its entirety. Nevertheless, I have tried to inject into our life here the element of stewardship without which the things that we love won't endure.'

In 2012, Scruton published *Green Philosophy: How to Think Seriously about the Planet*. It sought to show how the environment is best protected, not by global activism, but by local initiatives that inspire and are inspired by a love of home. It was a comprehensive defence of conservatism as the philosophy best placed to care for creation.[1] However, I put it to Scruton that it seems to have been overlooked by the left. 'Some do take an interest in it, but generally it is true that the book is not much referred to by left-leaning greens. It is unfashionable to treat the environment as a conservative cause, and unfashionable too to go through the arguments in this systematic way.

'When I do philosophy I like to be systematic, as in *The Aesthetics of Architecture* and *The Aesthetics of Music*. Similarly with *Green Philosophy*, I start from first principles, and try to establish what is available to us as rational beings by way of a motive to protect our environment, and where that motive would fit in with all the other things we have to reconcile with it. That is not how environmental activists tend to work. Their premise tends to be a large-scale panic: "Everything is totally and irreversibly threatened!" Having impressed that upon their readership, the next move is to say: "Therefore, we must change our way of life." They give formulae for doing the things that their readership wouldn't possibly be motivated to do, and then they conclude that since it is impossible, everything is coming to an end! People get excited by that. There's an area of the human psyche that is easy to visit in this way, with electrifying prophecies of doom. Factitious despair is a substitute for the moral life. Many young Muslims have discovered that it is easier to be a fanatic than to make compromises with those who disagree with you, because fanaticism is rooted in despair and doesn't demand a carefully negotiated and compassionate response to the existing problem.

'Nietzsche was surely right about resentment. People with advantages are easily targeted by those without them. You are never going to get rid of that motive because we are competitive, driven by what René Girard calls "mimetic desire". Some will succeed, and if some succeed then others, comparatively speaking, must fail. The seeds of resentment are therefore planted in the human condition. And much of green philosophy on the left seems to be an extension of resentment into this new realm of political interest, pinning the blame on those with money, property, land, industry and so on. Yet it could be that the environment is never better protected than by the wealthy, the landed and the privileged, for the reason that they are the ones with the greatest interest in passing things on. I wish sometimes that leftist environmentalists would rise to this challenge, and engage people like me in argument. But on the whole they do not do so. My book offers an extended and respectful criticism of George Monbiot's approach to environmental issues, and it would have been interesting to read his response to it. But there has been no response that I am aware of. Of course, George may think that my arguments are too paltry to merit a response, and God knows they are full of weaknesses.

'On the other hand, when I first moved here, and in the early days of our marriage, nearly twenty years ago, I did find myself in continuous and fruitful discussion with people on the left. I was deeply concerned about the future of the countryside under a Labour government and approached Anthony Barnett, a leftist supporter of the Labour Party and an old friend, with the suggestion that we set up a forum to discuss the relation between town and country in the emerging world. We established something called the Town and Country Forum, and would meet regularly in London, Sophie organizing a distinguished visitor speaking. This was a very enjoyable and instructive initiative, through which I made many new friends on both left and right. At a certain stage we published a volume of papers – *Town and Country* – some of which are classics of their kind.[2]

'Anthony introduced us to Ken Worpole, who invited Colin Ward, the extraordinary anarchist architect and town planner. Colin had been strongly influenced by Kropotkin and the philosophy of "mutual aid". His anarchism, founded as it was in respect for the little platoon and the spirit of cooperation, was not so very far from my conservatism. He reminded me too of my father, and in particular of the public-spirited love of the local and the attached which had mitigated my father's resentment and endowed him with the virtues of a citizen. The Town and Country Forum lasted a few years, and many of us keep in touch with each other. But it was unusual precisely in its attempt to lift environmental questions free from the rival ideologies, so that they could be considered as questions for us all.

'One of the people who attended the Town and Country Forum was the radio commentator and soil-loving farmer Robin Page, who has farmed all his life near Cambridge and who established the Countryside Restoration Trust with the intention of propagating his ideas for a healthier relation between farming and the land. He impressed on me that a vision of the land and its meaning is a necessary part of any mature political philosophy. I have also been influenced by Simon Fairlie, and his journal *The Land*. In so far as I have got involved in farming – and it is as yet not very far – it has been through the inspiration that they have provided.

'We have now begun to play our part in the local milk economy, raising some cows of our own. And Sophie has begun a business buying and selling the local cheeses that were once the substance of the North Wiltshire economy, but which have now to be revived *ab initio*. This is a marvellous opportunity to put into practice some of the principles explored in *Green Philosophy*, integrating husbandry and landscape protection, rural production and urban consumption, the cosmopolitan palate and the rustic activities that feed it. All this has deepened our attachment to this little piece of land, which is marked by so many of our most enjoyable days.'

To look at the land as Hegel might is to see it as something that reflects back our own image, our own spirit or consciousness – what he called *Geist*. That is because it is we who, in settling, have shaped, tended and moulded it in accordance with our own needs, using it too as a vehicle for self-knowledge. This, I point out, is very different from seeing the land as a quasi-divinity, which many on the left do. 'Yes, I am against that mournful Gaia hypothesis. However, I do believe that our sense of the sacred is one of our most profoundly positive ecological emotions. I take the example of Pausanias and his journey through Greece. He was very conscious of the way in which place after place had been consecrated either to heroes or to gods. The temples were still standing and the sacred groves had not been felled. Take away the temples and the consecrated battle fields, take away the signs of ancestral settlement, take away the right of inheritance and all the other forms in which the spirits of the departed still haunt the land – take them away and the motive to protect the land will disappear.'

Scruton the farmer married his second wife, Sophie Jeffreys, in 1996 and in 1998 they had Sam. How did this considerable transition alter his outlook on life and his philosophical vision? 'Many people undergo something like that. I had not expected to be quite as immediately taken up by marriage and family. However, I don't think it changed my writing or my thinking because it was so compatible with the way my thinking was going. Of course, it meant that I had very different kinds of human relations around me. A family is a completely different thing from intellectual friendships. You want to think it has changed you for the better, that you have become less selfish and so on, but I fear that I haven't been changed for the better! Certainly, making room for a wife and children in a life hitherto dedicated to purely creative and self-centred things involves a change in personality. But it is a question of whether you can do it successfully.'

For me, Scruton's writing certainly became somewhat gentler from the end of the 1990s. Did marriage and fatherhood contribute to this? 'Perhaps they did. My writing was going in that direction though, wasn't it? If you look at my *Xanthippic Dialogues*,[3] which is one of my favourite books, you will see there an attempt to put forward my social philosophy, and my philosophy of sex, in a way that is comparatively gentle and humorous.'

Talking of gentleness, I enquire about the title of Scruton's memoir *Gentle Regrets*, which was published in 2006 and ranks for many as one of his finest works. 'I thought that if I am to write about my past, I should include the element of regret, since I have had my share of it. I am not in favour of long biographies, which say everything irrelevant about their subject, and nothing relevant. But I had a collection of semi-autobiographical essays, in which I called upon my own experience, not because it was mine, but because it was an experience that seemed to illuminate a particular topic. So I assembled these chapters into something that would look like a portrait of their author. My editor at Continuum, Robin Baird-Smith, wanted me to write an autobiography, and this was the best I could do.

'I am not a heroic person. I don't claim to have made a great impression on the world or to have had a great task that I have fulfilled. I was not boasting about my achievements in writing that book, since there are very few of them, but pointing out that amid all the regrets and the disappointments, there were useful stories to tell. Because I am a risk-taker I have had a very interesting life, and among the most interesting things that have happened to me are the moments when I've been targeted by unremitting hostility. That is not pleasant, but it forced me into self-examination and into an apologetic attitude. I have always had this attitude in personal things, I think. Learning to apologize is the most important part of growing up, especially if you are rebellious and arrogant as I have surely been at times. I have felt the pressure throughout my life to distinguish the things for which I must apologize from the other things where I must stand up in a posture of defiance.'

I ask if his new life on the farm with Sophie, Sam and subsequently Lucy put his old life into a negative perspective. 'No, not really, because it was always a preparation for this. Sophie is an extremely generous person who looks back over my life without any kind of jealousy or vindictiveness. On the contrary, she finds it interesting. She has become very close friends with people with whom I've been intimate. It's not like Bartók's *Bluebeard's Castle*, where the latest wife enters the last room into which her predecessors have disappeared, thereafter never to be heard of again. On the contrary, sometimes I fear they will all cosy up in that last room and lock me out of it.'

Scruton met Sophie out hunting. 'On one of those mornings', he recounts in *On Hunting*, 'I was introduced to a quiet girl whose delicate features deeply appealed to me, and whose eyes seemed full of quizzical interest, as though surprised by light… A few weeks later, out hunting with the Beaufort, Barney lost his legs on a slippery corner and came crashing down. I retrieved the horse, and the hunt went on. But one person stayed behind to help me, losing precious minutes which might ruin her day, and that was Sophie. Alert, considerate and poised, she overcame with a few deft words my fear of hunting women. The crazy thought entered my head, that in these bright young eyes there shone a soul as pre-modern as mine.'[4]

It seems that Scruton's later years, those in which he found lasting love and finally settled in place where he is happy, are held together by hunting. 'That is too strong. But hunting undeniably changed my life, by creating another centre of being from which my projects radiate, and to which they return. But it didn't displace writing as my principal calling: writing is still what I have done every day. Hunting and farming gave me a new subject-matter. *On Hunting* and *News from Somewhere* are minor works of literature – but they are still works of *literature*, and not just the plodding ruminations of a failed academic. And Sophie is part of the reason for this: she is the "reality principle" to which my thoughts and feelings return. Although I had written novels and stories, these new books took my experience and captured it in words that others might have pleasure in reading. That was a big transition for me.'

News from Somewhere sought to capture the daily routine of farm life in and around the area where the Scrutons live. Did the neighbours about whom he wrote in that book actually read it? 'I don't raise the question with them, but I think they do read it and recognize themselves in the descriptions. But they keep their feelings to themselves. Others who are not immediately around here, but who live in the way I describe, have read both *News from*

Somewhere and *On Hunting*, and found consolation in them. That is because both books touch on their way of life and the place where they are.'

Do such people see Scruton as someone who champions their lives? 'Inevitably, I am called upon to talk to hunts and to encourage them at their annual general meetings. Rarely since Siegfried Sassoon has the hunting community had an intellectual spokesman, though it should be said that Jane Ridley fits the bill as well as I do.'

And what of rearing Sam and Lucy in a modern context: did Scruton find it difficult or were they protected on Sunday Hill Farm? 'Yes, our children were brought up in a fairly protected way. They did not have television until Sam was fourteen; they got it for the London Olympics. I regretted it coming but there was no resisting it by then, since both children were entirely familiar with television from their own explorations of the neighbourhood, and from visits to friends. They have not missed out on anything, because everything that we don't have here they can get through their schools and through the peer relationships that have developed there. They have a wide circle of friends, so they are not really confined to what the country can offer them. And what the country does offer them, which is horses and animals and all the excitement of living among farmers, is a bonus.

'On the whole, having children wasn't any interruption at all. Let's imagine that, for some reason, I had had the children and Sophie had disappeared and I had had to bring them up myself. I wouldn't have known what to do. Sophie has an instinct for it and is completely on their side, which I'm not. I am a mild but implacable enemy, who disapproves of everything they do. She is their alert and supportive friend. So they trust her and she's able to shape them as basically human, which I don't think I would have succeeded in doing. In fact their humanity and good nature constantly surprise me, and I ask myself what did I do to deserve this? And the answer is that I married Sophie.'

In all that he has said and written about Sophie, it seems that Scruton considers this a match made in heaven? 'No. It is a match very much made on earth. When I met Sophie I was lonely, bewildered, hoping to belong here below in a way that I hadn't really managed before. She straightforwardly loved me as a human being, didn't care so much about the "storm clouds in the intellectual sky" from which I was in flight, and did not idealize me, either positively, as an intellectual hero, or negatively, as a provocateur. To her I was just me. I came to earth in our marriage, though I don't deny that it was a blessing too. We share a love of horses and rural life. But there are many things we don't share. The intellectual life is not one to which Sophie is particularly adapted, even if she is at ease with my intellectual friends. But she loves adventure, and wants to make the world a better place, and that is an ambition that we share. And in everything there is, about her, a kind of poetry of which she is only half aware, and this is enough for me.'

Do Sam and Lucy read their father? 'I don't think so. *On Hunting* has been read. The rest is all above their heads at present. They did show great curiosity in *The Disappeared* but they've been forbidden to read it!' Are they conservatives or are they children of Cyberia? 'Oh, they're *total* conservatives, in just the way that horses are. I don't think they'll go through any repudiation of that.'

10

Sinful Pleasures

'I am more a workaholic than an alcoholic'

No visitor to Sunday Hill Farm can fail to see that enjoyment is, for Scruton, a vital part of living well, even if it must be tempered by dangerous adventures and costly forms of political involvement. In his book *I Drink Therefore I Am*, written in praise of wine, he expounds his philosophy of enjoyment at length, early on castigating the 'health fanatics' who wish to censor our pleasures:

In his essay on Persian poetry Emerson commends the great wino Hafiz in the following words:

> *Hafiz praises wine, roses, maidens, boys, birds, mornings and music, to give vent to his immense hilarity and sympathy with every form of beauty and joy; and lays emphasis on these to mark his scorn of sanctimony and base prudence.*
>
> It is against sanctimony and base prudence that much of my argument is directed, not in order to encourage vice, but in order to show that wine is compatible with virtue. The right way to live is by enjoying one's faculties, striving to like and if possible to love one's fellows, and also to accept that death is both necessary in itself and a blessed relief to those whom you would otherwise burden. The health fanatics who have poisoned all our natural enjoyments ought, in my view, to be rounded up and locked together in a place where they can bore each other rigid with their futile nostrums for eternal life. The

rest of us should live out our days in a chain of linked symposia, in which the catalyst is wine, the means conversation, the goal a serene acceptance of our lot and a determination not to outstay our welcome.[1]

This exuberant dismissal of the health lobby met, however, with a setback in 2002, when the *Guardian* newspaper published a leaked e-mail, sent by Sophie to people at Japan Tobacco International in Geneva, discussing the renewal of a monthly contract for advice on media relations. The e-mail delighted Scruton's enemies and opponents, since the wording seemed to suggest that he was being paid to place articles favourable to smoking. The resulting scandal, amplified by the media, led to a serious down-turn in what was already a downward-tending career. I ask Scruton to explain what happened, and whether it had not been a big mistake to get involved with the tobacco industry, notorious as it was for telling lies about its product.

'It was of course a big mistake to take money from a tobacco company, at a time when the industry had been effectively demonized. I was very naïve, and had wandered unwarily into a minefield. It happened this way: through the Eastern European consultancy which I described a while back I had got to know people who worked in the media relations office at JTI, which was a new firm that had just acquired the European branch of R. J. Reynolds Tobacco. Through no fault of their own they had been branded as pariahs, having acquired not only the assets but also the stigma of RJR, which had been a leading culprit in the attempt to deny the risks attached to smoking. Unfortunately the advertising bans meant that JTI had no way to make its presence known or to clear its name. Their main competitor, Philip Morris, has been a great supporter of advertising bans, which reinforce its monopoly position. They were therefore eager for a way of getting their product and their approach to it noticed.

'When we had established our media relations agency, with the Countryside Alliance as our first (and almost equally politically incorrect) client, JTI suggested funding us to organize the kinds of thing that they needed – meetings with journalists, and a publication that would ensure discussion of their issues, without being in any way construed as advertising or propaganda, which in the circumstances would obviously be counterproductive. We agreed, and that way Sophie and I were able to start work on what was, until disaster struck, one of the most agreeable of our commercial ventures – the *Risk of Freedom Briefing*.

'I was, at the time, beginning to work on environmental questions and had become very interested in the way in which risk, in modern societies, is being confiscated from those who would willingly undertake it, and controlled, serviced and taxed by the state. Increasingly we live in a risk-averse society which out-sources risk to government agencies, and lives in a cushioned but deeply insecure environment that could vanish at a single blow. We discussed these issues in our *Briefing*, and built up a circle of interesting people, including the geographer John Adams who had written brilliantly on risk, Claire Fox who went on to found the Battle of Ideas, the economist Tony Curzon-Price, Mick Hume, now of *Spiked*, and a range of friendly scientists and journalists, who would meet for lunch and discussion and often publish in our *Briefing* or elsewhere. It was all above board. Everybody attending our lunches was informed of the sponsor, I was named in the *Briefing* as editor and JTI as the sponsor, and we seldom if ever, as I recall, wrote about tobacco, relevant though that issue was. (You can find the many issues of the *Briefing* on the web.) I later drew on our discussions in the argument about risk and the law of unintended consequences, which forms a central strand of *Green Philosophy*. All in all it seemed harmless enough, and enabled us to employ a full-time secretary and to work on building up our business.'

I question whether it is right to run a media relations consultancy while also working as a journalist. The possible conflict of interest will always be looming. 'You are right,' Scruton responds at once. 'But I took the view – naïve and self-serving though it was – that it would be OK provided I was not influenced by our clients to publish what I would not otherwise have written. After all, I was a freelance journalist, with no contractual obligations. It should be said, however, that our firm was not a huge success, since we had no capital, and were running it from a shed in the garden at Sunday Hill Farm. We were not in a position to issue glitzy brochures or to invite CEOs onto the premises. We did acquire a few small clients, including a Dutch cancer charity seeking to explain its formula for living with cancer, and a supermarket hoping to brand itself as a purveyor of local food, as well as various small initiatives of an environmental kind. Our clients found my way of crafting messages very helpful in their publicity and press releases. Let's face it, anybody who has managed to make conservatism intellectually respectable must have a certain gift of persuasion.

'When the scandal broke we were very much on the back foot, and beaten down by the level and unscrupulousness of the assaults. I had not really grasped, until that moment, the extent of the enmity towards me, especially among journalists and activists. One person, connected to the anti-smoking charity ASH, pursued the cause to the limit, writing insinuating and malicious letters to everyone who might conceivably provide me with support or employment, including my department at Birkbeck College, and of course to editors of newspapers and the staff at JTI, pointing out how inadvisable it was to be associated with such a dubious person. He clearly worked day and night on this task, in gleeful triumph at the damage he was inflicting. Some of the letters came our way and we published a few in our *Briefing* – they are as near in style to the denunciations sent to the Gestapo as I could imagine. I was forced then to see myself from the outside, as someone whom a stranger could hate with a visceral loathing and also wish to destroy.

'The philosophy department at Birkbeck, without asking me to explain myself, removed my privileges as a visiting professor – something they could do because I was not a paid employee, and the editor of the *Financial Times* terminated my contract for a column on country living. The publisher Chatto & Windus, which had been negotiating for a book made from that column (a book which eventually appeared as *News from Somewhere*), wrote to cancel the deal, and for a moment it did look as though my career as a writer was at an end. JTI, however, to its credit, continued to fund the *Briefing* while we looked around for alternative methods of support, and friends began to step in to offer that support. One of those friends was Anthony Barnett who responded to the crisis with manly devotion, offering Sophie a job with Open Democracy, the webzine that he founded and which was, at the time, reasonably flush. Eventually the whole thing was reduced to a cloud of smoke adrift on the web, but not before we had decided that we could not really live with the hostility and should start a new life in America.'

I mention the fact that Scruton used to smoke himself. 'Yes, I used to smoke cigars, but I never liked it very much, and have always been conscious of the risks involved, the more so since becoming an expert, which was one effect of our work for JTI. On the other hand, we should recognize that, whatever the health costs, there are social benefits. Offering a cigarette is a very easy, relatively costless form of hospitality. For working people, it has had a huge social significance. Now that they can't do that, it's harder for them to get through barriers at work and also through their conflicts.'

Whether or not cigarettes help people to get through barriers, it has been a persistent theme of Scruton's writing that drink has just such a beneficial effect. *I Drink Therefore I Am* has been widely acclaimed for its beauty, humour and insight. I first came to realize how important wine is to the life of this thinker, when I read his column from *The Times* concerning white burgundy. 'Of all the conflicts that have shaken the civilised world,' he writes,

> that between claret and burgundy has probably been the most beneficial. It is at once easily resolved and endlessly renewable. It begins in pleasure and ceases in sleep, passing meanwhile through a glorious interlude of belligerent intoxication. Language, literature, history – all are brought to bear on this vital disputation, which has absorbed the after-dinner energies of countless politicians and businessmen, so stilling for a few precious hours the dangerous projects of production and reform.[2]

How did Scruton come to learn about wine to such a degree that he could write about it with such tenderness and ease? 'It isn't difficult, to be quite honest. If you really like wine you get fascinated by the labels. It's like train spotting: your real train spotter will be able to say immediately what make of engine that is, what that registration number means and so on. It is a skill you acquire very quickly and it is the same with wine. You remember the names on the bottle, you read about it and slowly it begins to fit together. I didn't find it difficult because it is knowledge that I have picked up over the years through leading a serious drinking life. You must also recognize that, in a world of global and globalized consumption, wine is the last genuinely local product – the last product that comes to you labelled with its origins, and esteemed for its origins and all the meaning that attaches to them.'

Writing is a lonely enterprise and it deserves its rewards at the end of the day. Did wine help fortify Scruton against the loneliness that inevitably comes with being a serious writer? 'Oh yes, certainly. I don't deny that wine is a health risk. But I am lucky to have a constitution that enables me to drink every day. At the end of each day, even if I have got no company there is still a glass in my hand. I am more a workaholic than an alcoholic, so the alcohol is the reward for the work. Also, as I was saying, it is very important that we have things that we can offer to each other – things that produce some immediate psychic effect and which enable us to step out of the urgencies of daily life into some more relaxed arena where we can encounter people in another mood.

'I think that is why all societies have some intoxicant or other that is the received form of small-scale hospitality. It's also why I think Western societies, and America in particular, have been so successful at adapting to new forms of business and new ways of earning a living. The creative nature of the Western economy has a lot to do with the fact people can break the ice straight away at a cocktail party. All business conferences begin in this way, and, by the end of the evening, bonding has occurred of a kind that wouldn't occur over the desk in the daytime or through a business correspondence. The absence of alcohol from Saudi Arabia is one reason why it has stayed so solidly locked in its joyless sterility, dependent for its wealth on fossil fuels, and for its stability on its fossilized religion.'

For Scruton, wine highlights our transcendental dimension or, as he writes in *I Drink Therefore I Am*: 'Through wine we know, as through almost nothing else that we consume, that we are one thing, which is also two: subject and object, soul and body, free and bound.' I ask him to elaborate on this Kantian aspect of wine drinking for me. 'I was once talking to a friend who became a colleague, and who had been my PhD student, about this very issue. She visited me and I opened a bottle of wine, as she argued that the Kantian concept of the thing-in-itself can be given only a negative interpretation. "There are limits to what can be known; we can know the world through experience, but our attempts to get behind the veil of appearance, from the phenomenon to the noumenon, are bound to fail. So what positive knowledge of the things themselves is available?" And I said to her: "Look, you drink that glass of wine and compare your knowledge of it after you've absorbed it with your knowledge of it before. Then you will see the kind of thing Kant had in mind: there is a knowledge of things from within that comes to us in another way, and wine is a symbol of this. You can't say in any words what it is that has been added by this experience, but when you swallow you know the wine in another way. It is like that when suddenly we see the world from God's perspective, as only accidentally revealed in space and time." So she swallowed the wine and exclaimed: "By God, you're right!"

'That said, I don't think wine actually does bring us across the threshold to the transcendental; it merely gives us a sense of what it *would* be like, suddenly to view from within what we normally understand only from without. Music is different and this is where Schopenhauer is so interesting. He not only thinks that music takes us across the threshold, but he has a theory to explain what the threshold is between appearance and thing-in-itself. It is the threshold between the world of representation and the world of will. It is not necessary to accept Schopenhauer's metaphysics of the will in order to discern a measure of truth in what he says. Our thinking stops of necessity at the bounds of sense; but it is essentially aimed beyond them. The German idealists all fluttered around this thought like moths around a light, but finding the right language to express it is not easy.

'You get to the limit with words and with scientific enquiry, but you feel there is a beyond which you can somehow engage with. Music is like a language, but it isn't impeded in the same way that language is by the need for conceptualization and answerability to truth conditions. So it naturally becomes a symbol of the thing that wants to be said but cannot be said. And the very fact that music is also an utterance that we sing out and put ourselves into reinforces this suggestion. Therefore we ask ourselves whether music, if properly treated, could get across that threshold, or at least give us the sense of what it's like on the other side. My view is that the contrapuntal grammar of our music brings voices together on the edge of things. It gives you a sense of standing on that edge, looking away from the world out towards the transcendental. Of course, you can't say in words what it is that you perceive or know.

'All such experiences can be interpreted as referring, not to a beyond, but to some feature of this world – to your own fantasies and projections. The question is whether you can distinguish those things which are *mere* projections from those things which are, as Wordsworth would put it, *intimations* of the beyond or of the mysterious reality of the world. All mystics and religious people think that there is that distinction. In his great essay on art and religion, Wagner thinks that art does this for you – that it takes you to the point where you *can* make the distinction between the mere projection and the spiritual reality, even though this reality lies in you.'

With the mass marketing of wine, the experience of this drink as an intimation of the transcendental has been lost to many. How does Scruton react to this? 'Going back to Hegel, experiences don't necessarily have meaning prior to our putting meaning into them. But when we put meaning into them, we are also trying to understand them. In the old days, when wine was a precious thing and the dusty bottle was brought up from the cellar, the first whiff of wine in the cold English air was like Stefan George's "breeze from other planets". The ceremonial aspect of tasting was an attempt to impart meaning to what might otherwise be void of it. The case is no different from that of hunting as I described it earlier. Here too Yeats's suggestion is borne out, that innocence and beauty are born of custom and ceremony. When wine becomes a mass-marketed product it becomes so much harder to build into the experience of drinking it a true sense of its preciousness.

'In sum, we build meaning into our experiences, but we can only do so if they already have the valency that makes this possible. And the meanings that make things matter are those that we build when we're together. You can, of course, drink on your own, but it is true of all intoxicants that the search for the meaning that they contain is a social search. It is something that people do together.

'On the other hand, meaning is always at risk when it is too easily available. It's like music: when you can turn it on anywhere and it sounds in your ears as you walk down the street, that sense of its preciousness, of its apartness from everyday life, has been taken away.'

Scruton takes me to his wine store to collect a few bottles. He tells me that he is not a collector. Not only can he not afford it, but the expertise of the wine connoisseur, he argues, is more or less entirely phoney. This is especially so in the matter of Sauternes, he adds, a bottle of which he has singled out for the evening's symposium. 'Appreciation of this wine is in no way helped by chattering in winespeak. Of course, it helps to know how it is produced, and where – namely on the banks of the Garonne where the Ciron flows into it, bringing the chill mountain waters from the Pyrenees. That creates the mist that stimulates the "noble rot", so shrivelling the grapes. It is not surprising if the result is expensive – though no more expensive than it deserves to be.'

Sam chuckles at his father's almost reverent description of the 'noble rot', and persists in repeating the phrase throughout the evening. For Scruton, however, Sauternes is something that ought to be taken very seriously, precisely because the cult of the collector has made it possible to acquire really good examples at comparatively low cost. Collectors, he points out, have been won over by winespeak, so as to believe that Château d'Yquem is a kind of work of art, a bargain at any price. But, as he writes in *I Drink Therefore I Am*,

> Yquem has absolutely no market among real wine lovers. If they have enough money for a bottle of Yquem, they will buy half a dozen Ch. Suduiraut ... or Lafaurie-Peyraguey instead. Yquem can maintain its price only because the world is full of stinking rich vulgarians who know nothing about wine, and therefore buy the best ...
>
> There are those who are distressed when rich people spend hundreds, sometimes even thousands of pounds on a bottle of wine, while others are obliged to drink water. But if you have a lot of money,

throwing it away is best – best for you, since it frees you of a burden, best for the recipient, who needs it more than you do (else why are you throwing it away?), best for all of us, who are somewhere downstream from your folly. And the more perishable and pointless the thing on which your money is squandered, the more worthy the act. The worst use of money is to add to the junk pile of old cars or kitsch houses. The best use is to buy mega-expensive wine, so turning your money into biodegradable urine, and returning it to the primordial flux.[3]

We savour the wine with Scruton's friend David Wiggins and his wife. And then we finish with whisky, a drink with which Scruton sometimes likes to wash down the day. Years ago, after we had shared a glass in my home in Dublin, he sent me this tender reflection, one of many columns written during his stint as wine critic for the *New Statesman*, part of which coincided with his time living in rural Virginia:

'If ah git to Heav'n, then fust thing ah do is shake that man's han' as invented whiskey.' Only in rural America will you hear a remark like that. I suggest that whiskey was not invented by a single person, but emerged, as Adam Smith would say, by an 'invisible hand'. 'Well, ah gonna shake that han' too.' 'Amen,' adds the chorus, for we are in Southern Baptist country, and God's ears are pricked. I question whether an interest in whiskey would survive the passage through the Pearly Gates, to which I receive the sensible reply: 'so why did He get us all so innerested in whiskey down here?' God has a lot to answer for in old Virginia.

And answer He does. Sitting on the porch after sundown, listening to the tree frogs trilling and the land frogs squeaking, I remind God to ensure that a cask or two of our local rye is on tap when He meets the neighbours. They're sure gonna need it. Meanwhile, I raise my glass. For there is no better place to drink whiskey than on a southern porch at night-time, the warm air bristling with insects, the bats swooping under the eaves and every now and then the sky tearing like paper as an owl rips past. Yes, and those tree frogs or tree toads, as Walt

Whitman called them: 'a chef d'oeuvre for the highest' – though the highest what, he did not say. If only it were a little less lonely; and then behold, in answer to my prayer, Dolly the collie comes bounding up the steps and lays her rag-doll body at my feet.

Dolly's owner, who lives alone in a cabin on the hill, still feeds her. But she stops in to see him only when her stomach complains. Otherwise she is here, asleep on the porch, hunting in the plantation, or dashing across the river in pursuit of racoons, possums and deer. Last week she was sprayed by a skunk, and the acrid smell still lingers. Her flesh is knobbly with ticks, and her matted fur is home to a thousand smaller parasites. Yet her cheerful presence is comforting beyond words and I fetch some water so that we can drink together. The sound of the dog-tongue lapping in the bowl reminds me of the ease with which we humans can buy the affection of animals. And that in turn reminds me to count my blessings.

Yes, whiskey is certainly one of them. Its grainy bitterness, its nutty aroma, its long tail of fire like a comet as it hurtles through the dark – all these things have a magic of their own, and both liven the body and bring it to rest. As I settle down to enjoy the night, I look at Dolly, and see on her bright piebald face the very same contentment that I feel behind my own. And for a brief moment I am conscious of what I have lost, in needing whiskey, not water, for my peace of mind.

I recall those words as I lower the glass and head upstairs to 'settle down and enjoy the night'. But then, from my room above his study, I hear my host playing Wagner on the piano. In such moments, Scruton demonstrates his need constantly to return to the places where, if he is right, the transcendental can be glimpsed on some inaccessible horizon.

11

Rediscovering Religion

'I think this life is probably enough'

As we resume our conversations on Monday morning, I recall our visit to All Saints Church in the parish of Garsdon for Palm Sunday service. Garsdon is four miles to the east of Malmesbury, and All Saints sits on a hill overlooking the surrounding countryside. Roger plays the organ at this church, which is a beautiful remnant of old England, though one with interesting American connections, since Garsdon was the seat of the Washington family, and the church still contains one of their memorials. As I sat listening to him play a repertoire of traditional and modern hymns, I recalled this passage from *England: An Elegy*:

> Thus the hymnal, like the Bible, has helped to unite the Anglican and Nonconformist churches. The hymns have been shaped by the liturgy; but they in turn have shaped the service of the Anglican Church. They have provided the important moments of participation, in which God is praised and worshipped in song, and the drama of the service is momentarily interrupted by the chorus. They have replaced the psalms as vehicles of collective sentiment, and the psalms in their turn have become part of the liturgy.[1]

Despite having 'served an apprenticeship in atheism', Scruton has, I suggest, never been an atheist per se. 'On the contrary, I have always assumed that religion is necessary to human communities on sociological and anthropological grounds, as well as on metaphysical grounds. People need something with which to root their beliefs, and also their conduct, their sense of themselves and their relation to others. We are fundamentally related beings and all the religions are shaped by this great need. Take religion away and nihilism is the first result, and then chaos, which is what we're seeing now. That, of course, doesn't mean that the doctrines are true. This is the great difficulty for people like me who begin from that anthropological sense of what religion is: how do we make the Kierkegaardian "leap of faith" into the actual affirmation of a doctrine? That is something with which I have wrestled all my life.'

When did this wrestling begin? 'It was a "puberty moment". When, as a boy, I went in secret to the Anglican Church, I was affirming my own independence and my incipient love of the English way of doing things. But that didn't last: my life was very soon swept into disorder by the need to leave home and to fend for myself. At Cambridge, I *did* become fairly atheistical and I have since been persuaded that the truth about our world is given by science and not by any theological doctrine. That is what science is: an attempt to give the truth about our world. It can make no place for the "divine hypothesis". One must therefore find another, non-scientific way to resuscitate the basic contours of a religious worldview, and that is really what I have been doing in my writings. I share with Richard Dawkins the image of the completeness of the natural sciences and the view that there isn't anything that they leave unexplained, other than the great fact that there is something, and not nothing, a fact that is for that reason inexplicable. Nevertheless, the natural sciences do not give a full description of the things with which they deal.

'I have been very influenced in this by Wagner, and by his attempt, not just to show that art gives you an alternative approach to the deep truths about the human condition that religion advances, but also that it enables you, to a great measure, to resuscitate the idea of the sacred – which is the idea upon which human communities ultimately depend. The sacred is something which one has to find in one's own life if one is to live that life correctly. So that's the thought that I have been working towards, and in *The Soul of the World* I connect this with a "cognitive dualism" that allows the universalist pretensions of science while withdrawing from the idea that science tells us the whole truth and the ultimate truth.'

One of the ways in which Scruton has sought to withdraw from the idea that the universalist pretensions of science contain the ultimate truth is by putting a human face on things. What precisely does this involve? 'As I have said, I was brought up in analytical philosophy at Cambridge, a school descended from John Locke. Locke described philosophy as the "handmaiden of the sciences", the idea being that the philosopher doesn't himself make any contribution to our knowledge of the world. Rather, he clarifies the language and the arguments with which we conduct our scientific investigations. That is the ultimate assumption of the analytical philosophers and I've never been happy with it. I've always thought of philosophy in the old Platonic way as the attempt to find a comprehensive picture of what we are, of where we are and of how we are. This search promises to show the human being as something that isn't strange, and to enable us to face the peculiarities of our condition and adopt them as our own.

'Most people are in flight from the difficult realities. Religion helps them to arrest this flight. It turns them around again towards the light, so that they see life whole, and lift their eyes from the shadows. But when you haven't got that religious certainty, you still need something else if you are to see things as they are and not be frightened by them. I think of philosophy as doing that.'

I put it to Scruton that Kant was doing something similar when, despite his affirmation of science, he sought to protect the transcendental from a purely mechanistic worldview. 'Kant was a very special case. For the first time, he used philosophy both to justify science and to set limits to it. This was a remarkable achievement. Having done that, he was very aware that, when the limits had been drawn, there was something left over. But he wisely maintained that the thing left out is not some realm of non-scientific fact, but a realm beyond the factual altogether: the Kingdom of Ends. That is the realm of practical reasoning. And so he founded his vision of human salvation on a theory of the moral law and human freedom – a theory which is majestic in its ambition but also hard to grasp. So yes, that has been the model for my own philosophy, which sees the world as enclosed within a one-sided boundary. Like flies at a window, we gather at the edge. But the light in that window comes from nowhere that we could visit, not even in thought.'

Why does he think that, despite Kant and his descendants, scientism has become such a phenomenon? 'In our time, scientific advance has been enormous and it is no longer possible to think that science is going to stop short of giving a full explanation of everything. It *will* give a full explanation of everything, but it will be an explanation that will be extremely hard to understand. The more science comprehends, the more abstract and mathematical are its premises. That is intimidating; philosophers don't dare to speak against the authority of science because it is so extraordinarily potent in its ability to ask and answer questions. The history of philosophy is littered with pseudo-science. So for many of our philosophical colleagues in Britain and America science is treated as impregnable. There is no way you can criticize it from a philosophical perspective, even if something like Kant's thesis is right.'

I suggest that Scruton himself is surely not one of those who think that science is impregnable, and that he often does dare to speak outside its authority. A prime example of this is the following:

> Science has its proselytisers and tub-thumpers – people who tell us that God is now redundant, and should be peaceably or forcibly retired. The smallest dose of philosophy would cure mankind of this delusion. All that science can show us is the *how* of God's creation; never can we by scientific means disprove the *fact* of it, still less cast light on the *why*. But the answer to the why lies here and now, in you and me – in the free and reflective being...[2]

'It is true that I would distinguish science from *scientism*. I don't follow Paul Feyerabend in imagining that scientific theories can be invented as one might wish. Science aims at objective truth and there is always the possibility that a currently accepted theory will be refuted: it wouldn't be a scientific theory if that possibility weren't there. Our knowledge of the world slowly increases through the application of the scientific method. Science aims to explain everything completely, in terms of the laws of motion that govern how things change. But it does not aim to answer every question – certainly not the question how to live, or the question why a law-governed universe exists in the first place (which might also be the last place).

'Scientism is a completely different thing. It arises when people take hold of fragments of science and rewrite the questions that trouble them in the language of those fragments. They then assume that they have found a solution. A very obvious example is "neurobabble", which takes hold of the embryonic scientific theory about the workings of the nervous system and uses it to re-describe the questions of consciousness and human action – all the things that philosophers puzzle over. Neurobabble describes all that we think, feel and do in terms of imaginary circuits in the brain, digital processing of data, the binary arithmetic of the synapse and so on. It then assumes that it has shown how the mind works, and that only a few clean-up operations remain before we have a complete account of human cognitive psychology. But the real question was begged from the beginning, which is the question whether the terms of that as yet merely imagined science apply to the workings of consciousness. I think scientism is always like that: it takes scientific terminology and applies it in advance of having shown that this terminology is relevant to the question. You find a version of this in the French frauds like Jacques Lacan and Alain Badiou, who borrow the jargon of mathematics in order to create an illusory sense of mastery over problems that they lack the ability to define.'

Even within the scientific community there are many who believe, like Scruton, that the question of consciousness is not one that can be solved. Elsewhere he has written:

The evangelical atheists are subliminally aware that their abdication in the face of science does not make the universe more intelligible, nor does it provide an alternative answer to our metaphysical enquiries. It simply brings enquiry to a stop. And the religious person will feel that this stop is premature: that reason has more questions to ask, and perhaps more answers to obtain, than the atheists will allow us. So who, in this subliminal contest, is the truly reasonable one? The atheists beg the question in their own favour, by assuming that science has all the answers. But science can have all the answers only if it has all the questions; and that assumption is false. There are questions addressed to reason which are not addressed to science, since they are not asking for a causal explanation. One of these is the question of consciousness… The great tapestry of waves and particles, of fields and forces, of matter and energy, is pinned down only at the edges, where events are crystallised in the observing mind.[3]

I urge Scruton to elaborate more on this question of consciousness. 'I think it is certainly true that this is a paradigm of a philosophical question that is not going to yield to scientific enquiry. But many philosophers get it wrong because they think of consciousness itself as the problem. The actual problem is subjectivity, self-consciousness and the first-person case. The consciousness of a dog is not a problem: it is a natural phenomenon like every other aspect of the dog's behaviour. But in my recent work, like *The Face of God*[4] and *The Soul of the World*, I have argued, as Kant argued in his lectures on anthropology, that we are distinguished from every other item in the universe by our ability to say "I". That ability is a mystery. And it is there that one has to begin the process of showing that there is another form of understanding, which is intrinsic to our self-knowledge, our knowledge of others and our relations to others. Doing that is the real task of philosophy.'

So will this mystery of subjectivity always be the limit that science cannot breach? 'What is astonishing about the physical sciences is the way in which, as you work back from theory to theory, there seems to be nothing left in the end except a collection of equations. That raises a huge question in the mind of everybody, scientists included, as to how the universe could possibly be like that. Is that a meaningful question? Kant would say that if it is a question asked from within science, then the only answer to it is that this is how things are. But if it's a question asked from beyond the limit of science, then it immediately takes on a theological character and the question is whether there is such a thing as a theological answer. And that is where philosophy kicks in.'

Surely, for most ordinary people, that sense of the mystery of self-consciousness and subjectivity is encapsulated in religion. But what happens to that sense when, as is now the case, religion declines? 'This is the great difficulty. Ordinary people are not philosophers; they don't see things in the way I have been describing. It is undeniable that they do have a sense of mystery. Everybody is looking for something that explains why they are here and how they should lead their life. They are looking for a set of instructions and religion provides that. It also vindicates the life of prayer, vindicates ordinary morality and teaches humility. In all that, it fills in the gaps that science leaves open. So, ordinary people living a religious life are, in a sense, completed in a way that they wouldn't be if they just lived according to the nihilistic worldview that our culture advocates. In that sense, religion brings them nearer to the truth about their condition than they would otherwise be.

'But they don't think this through philosophically, and the philosopher thinking about these things might have a very different perception. He might think that many of the religious doctrines are myths or ritualistic pronouncements. There is a concealed truth within them, but it is one that ordinary people may not understand. This thought was already there in Averroes in Andalusian Spain. He said that there are reasons for religious doctrines, which can be presented with difficulty to the enquiring mind. Yet you should never reveal these reasons to ordinary people because the only result of this will be to remove their faith. Therefore, there have to be two parallel routes to the thing we call "religion": there has to be the religion of the philosopher, and the religion of the ordinary faithful. The philosopher might be judged heretical by the faithful because, by defending their certainties, he opens the door to doubt.'

I point out that, in most cases, the enquiring mind will move from religion to philosophy and then lose religion. However, in Scruton's case, he moved from philosophy to a position where he came to appreciate just how important religion is. 'Yes, that's exactly right: I went the other way. This is also the way Kierkegaard went. Ultimately, he recognized that the grounds of all religious belief are within the self, and that religion contains the set of stories that encapsulate our self-understanding. In that way, he was not very different from Wagner. However, he then went on to say that this doesn't mean that religion is without authority, because truth is subjectivity, and subjectivity is the *real* truth. In the *Concluding Unscientific Postscript*, he praised himself for being unscientific and thought he was nearer to the truth by making the question of truth entirely subjective. That is what I would call a philosophical failure, a retreat from truth rather than an encounter with it. You have to accept that truth is objectivity and not subjectivity. You have to accept that the scientific worldview is aiming to tell you how the world really is. This is where analytical philosophy is so important. We know from Frege and Tarski that truth is connected with reference, that reference is connected to identity and that identity determines our ontological commitments. Ultimately, therefore, you cannot avoid the scientific realist worldview: it is simply a consequence of logical thinking.

'That said, there was something very profound in what Kierkegaard said when he distinguished the aesthetic from the ethical and the religious forms of life. He saw the aesthetic not simply as a realm of experience only, but as a way of being in the world. And through that way of life, one comes to an understanding of man's spiritual condition – an understanding that is focused on self-gratification. The ethical or the moral is a growing up from that, in which relationships, institutions, long-term commitment and responsibility take over. In the religious experience the opposition between the aesthetic and the ethical is transcended and reconciled, since that is what the encounter with the sacred ultimately is – a fusing of the experience of beauty with the sense of moral order. That said, the best things that Kierkegaard wrote are in the first volume of *Either/Or*, on the aesthetic way of life. The essay on Mozart's *Don Giovanni* and 'The Diary of a Seducer' are, in themselves, terrific works of art. The essay on *Don Giovanni* is the first great piece of musical criticism by a philosopher.'[5]

I remark that Nietzsche accepted the scientific worldview, albeit in his own unique way. 'Yes, in his own way. Like everyone else at that time, he was profoundly shocked by Darwin, by the vision of the human being as an animal whose place in nature is not substantially different from that of any other animal. I never really know what to make of Nietzsche because one sentence will be profound and the next one will be shallow and even silly. In my view, he didn't grow up at all.'

Despite his reduction of the human being to a clever animal, didn't Nietzsche also sense something of the greatness of our condition? 'Yes, but he said, famously, that we have art so that we should not die of the truth – the "truth" being what science tells us: that we are just this *thing*, and art being the continuous attempt to construct another world in which we are redeemed by our freedom, and not simply this *thing*. He sought salvation from the real in a world of the imagination. That is, again, so close to Wagner.'

Even while serving his 'apprenticeship in atheism', when he was promoting what he once called a 'godless conservatism', Scruton still had a religious sensitivity. *Sexual Desire* places the sexual experience in a context that admits the religious worldview, and he would trenchantly criticize the naturalistic view of man in *The Philosopher on Dover Beach*. Still, he had not returned to the Christian Church, the reasons for which I now ask him to explain. 'My relationship with the Christian Church has always been tenuous. When I was living in France, I was fascinated by the village churches all around and by the celebration of Mass. I felt that this was a moment of beauty in lives that were not necessarily full of such moments. When Vatican II occurred I was shocked by it – especially by the damage done to the liturgy. Of course, I had an aesthetic rather than a religious view of the Church, but I saw Vatican II in slightly Spenglerian terms, as a movement of cultural degeneration. I didn't see why the reforms were necessary. I longed for the Church to be there, maintaining its liturgy and its presence as a holy thing on the edge of life, a rock on the far horizon against which the waves of fashion beat in vain. However, it was now disintegrating and there seemed to be no safety at all on the sea of life.

'Being around those Catholic churches also stimulated my interest in architecture. When I went to Rome, before going back to Cambridge to do research, the thing that interested me most was the Baroque style, and I tried to understand what people like Borromini and Bernini wanted to express through their vivid forms. Borromini was a huge influence on my thinking, not through his writings because there's nothing much there, but through his designs. *Why* he was doing what he was doing was an intellectual question. And the question was connected, for me, with the experience of these buildings as offering a kind of definition of the creator God. Borromini was giving objective form to a religious experience, and building this experience not only up into the dome but down into the details, so that every moulding and every shadow spoke of a world ordered towards the good. This you see especially in the church of S Carlino at the Quattro Fontane.'

I remind Scruton that he once said that Michelangelo's *Pietà* changed his life. Why? 'Michelangelo presented something absolutely fundamental in a way that I had not encountered before. He showed suffering itself as sacred and as a vehicle for redemption. The human body, through its vulnerability, offers a glimpse of immortality, and this is connected with the deepest things in us: love of mother and father, love of child, the protectiveness that flows from flesh to flesh – attachment in its primordial form.'

This leads me to ask if the world of art could have evolved without the Christian faith. 'All art is praise, Ruskin wrote. At least, all art of any value is praise. And whether or not praising God the artist must still assume a religious posture. The Christian religion has shaped our way of praising things. It provided our iconography in the visual arts, our syntax in architecture and the tradition of polyphony in music. Why is there so little real music coming out of the Islamic world? Surely it is because there is no polyphony in Islam. The culture is saying only *one* thing, a huge unison which constantly fragments and can restore itself only by violence.

'After the Reformation, the visual arts lost their iconography and painters turned to still life and to landscape painting. Dutch still life has a very Protestant feel to it, sanctifying ordinary things in their domestic uses, rather than pretending to offer glimpses of the transcendental. The monasteries and mysteries are now in the past: instead we have *this*, the fullness of living, eating and drinking together, and the law and industry that endow our objects with the only permanence they can enjoy, which is the permanence of ownership. Bach is the greatest composer who has ever lived, and his Protestantism is absolutely integral to his art. The centre of consciousness shifted in his day from Italy and the Catholic Mass to Germany and the Merchant City. True, he wrote a mass in B Minor, and very great it is. But his voice is the voice of the individual, meeting others contrapuntally, and each worshipping God in his own way.'

Does he believe the Reformation was a good or a bad thing? 'I can't really say whether it was good or bad, but it produced wonderful civilizations like Protestant Germany. It also produced absolute chaos in the Thirty Years War.' Yes, but didn't it produce the very same type of thing that he bemoaned in Vatican II? 'Yes, I know which side I would have been on in that battle, there's no doubt about it! But human beings are imperfect and competitive. Their default position is killing each other, that bleak confrontation with the void that Tolstoy describes, through Pierre's witnessing the worst of war, as 'It'. The best we can ever hope for in any major transformation is a compromise. Once 'It' had made itself known, once Luther had put his self-centred pronouncement on the door of the cathedral, it became inevitable that there would be murderous conflict. As a conservative, I would say the thing to do in such circumstances is to save what you can of the old thing, and reconcile it, if you can, to the new. That is what Anglicanism did. The new thing might be kitsch, like the post-Vatican II liturgy, which was an *unnecessary* response to a non-conflict. But the Anglican liturgy was an absolutely necessary response to a real conflict which, after a few burnings and beheadings, produced a sort of normality.'

The English Reformation did not emerge from the same set of circumstances as that in Germany. It was a personal issue which brought it about. Without that issue, would the Reformation still have been inevitable? 'As you know, we had a monarch who needed a male heir and who led a chaotic life. He was an extremely cruel and dominating character. But Calvinism had already taken root in Scotland, and the Reformation, in some form or other, would have been inevitable also here. The real question then was not whether the Church of England would become Protestant, but whether it would be Lutheran or Calvinist. The Anglican compromise was a marvellous way of preventing anybody from accusing it of being anything at all.'

In his writings on this subject, notably *Our Church: A Personal History of the Church of England*, Scruton seems to suggest that England was somehow always waiting for the Anglican religion: 'I think it was incipient in the Middle Ages in the conflict around the Constitutions of Clarendon which were issued by Henry II in 1164, and opposed by the Archbishop of Canterbury, Thomas à Becket. It was by then already clear that the English were Christian *in their own way* and had been since Saxon times. Their churches, and their Christian literature – think of *Piers Plowman* – indicate that Christianity had, in this country, already been wound together with the experience of this very special place, its climate, its landscape and the forms of life that had grown in its sheltered valleys. Here we are, our ancestors told themselves, on an island of our own, vulnerable to invasion from barbarians. Let us at least worship in our own way, since then we will stick together and be protected. The faith was adapted to the country, which was itself adapted to the faith. To some extent that kind of accommodation between faith and sovereignty goes on everywhere, but I think it went on especially in England, long before the Peace of Westphalia, when Europe as a whole first understood that nationality and religion must be wound together if they are not to destroy each other.'

On Palm Sunday, I heard Scruton play the organ at Garsdon church, but I had also witnessed him participating fully in the liturgy. Having long graduated from his apprenticeship in atheism, he is obviously now very much at home in this rather beautiful little chapel and among its quiet congregation. While we were there, he was approached by a parishioner who told him that he had returned to Sunday service after reading *Our Church*. But why had Scruton returned? 'I have always had spells when I really wanted to attend the Church. For a long time after my divorce from Danielle, I would go to a Catholic church or an Orthodox church for prayerful moments. I had no clear doctrinal commitment, only a deep sense of contrition, which could be relieved in no other way. When I came to settle here, it seemed quite natural to go to that little church of ours. And when I discovered that they hadn't an organist I decided to volunteer. This means that I am there every Sunday. Bit by bit, I sensed that a kind of faith can grow without the scaffolding of doctrine. The most important truths contained in the liturgy are not expressible in words. T. S. Eliot's pilgrimage is very like mine: he came to earth in belief.'

Still, the question remains as to what appeals to Scruton in Christianity? Is it the fact that God is revealed as a person, and it is precisely upon the notion of personhood and subjectivity that Scruton bases so much of his writing? 'That is true, although it doesn't distinguish Christianity from Islam or from Judaism. What appeals to me is the way in which the central mystery – of God incarnate *in* a human person – connects Him to the supreme act of sacrifice. I think that this undergoing of death on our behalf is a profound thing. To know that we share this with God Himself is what reconciles us to death. But I am sceptical about the Resurrection and the afterlife. In my book *Perictione in Colophon*,[6] Perictione, who leads Kierkegaard's aesthetic way of life, makes the remark that you only live once, and most people not even that much. And she is determined at least to live once. I think that is what one should do. But one can only do it if one does recognize the absolute importance in our lives of moments of sacrifice, and the fact that we are seeking redemption and can only find it if God too is prepared as a sacrifice. That is a mystical thing, wonderfully conveyed by Wagner in *Tristan and Isolde*, in which there is no suggestion of an afterlife, but only the great darkness in which you become what you truly are, which is nothing.'

But doesn't Scruton's transcendental threshold require the same type of faith practised by those who *do* believe in the Resurrection and the afterlife? 'Of course, it requires a lot of faith. It requires the view that there is a perspective on us and our world which is not ours and not available in this world. This is the God's-eye perspective, and from that perspective it really matters what we do.' It seems to me that this perspective of pure subjectivity, unencumbered by place and time, is that towards which Scruton is trying to move. 'Yes exactly, but also to feel the radiance of sympathy from that perspective.'

In his most recent writings on religion, Scruton has argued that even those who deny the transcendental presuppose it. I ask him to expand on this. 'What I really want to say is that it is presupposed in the first-person case. I consider Patricia Churchland's argument that neuroscience will replace what she calls "folk psychology", so as to tell us what we *really* are, replacing the illusory theory that we have been using up to now. Suppose, however, that we establish that pain is activity of the C fibres firing in a certain way. If that is a true identity statement then you are not entitled to make it unless you have the evidence for it. Therefore, you can only ever say you are in pain after you have done a lot of elaborate scientific research, looking into your own brain with whatever device you have for doing this. But this is one area where you can't make mistakes. And even if you did try to find out that you are in pain that way, you would end up saying something like: "My C fibres are firing, so it seems to *me* that I am in pain." All you have done in this case is to replace one first-person statement with another. The subjective perspective on the world is always there. As Sartre says, this subjective perspective is a *nothingness*. You can never turn around and grasp it because it is always behind you, ready of an instant to take up another position out of view.'

So, once they say 'me', the door opens for Scruton to come in? 'Once they say "I", the truth about their condition comes in. This is the only point where you can insert the subjective reality into scientific discourse, but it is also the point that scientific discourse cannot touch. Kant was right when he said that the ability to say "I" is tied up with human freedom, expressed through practical reason and the language of "ought". I have always been less interested in refuting what people like Churchland believe than in developing the alternative. It is, however, extremely difficult to find the way back to what Fichte and Hegel perceived about the self, without getting lost in their jargon and that peculiar dialectical way of arguing, which is really a way of avoiding argument. In this regard, Eliot's *Four Quartets* is worth twenty volumes of Hegel, because instead of trying to "eff" the ineffable, he presents it through images which cannot be spelled out as arguments but only absorbed as experiences.'

In *Gentle Regrets*, Scruton writes that 'my years as a voyeur of holiness brought me … into contact with true believers, and taught me that faith transfigures everything it touches, and raises the world to God. To believe as much is not yet to believe; but it is to know your insufficiency. And that knowledge has much in common with faith.'[7] One such true believer was Monsignor Alfred Newman Gilbey, who, as described by Scruton, 'had been Catholic chaplain in Cambridge during my undergraduate days … He had refurbished the chaplaincy in the style of a counter-reformation shrine, had searched assiduously for undergraduates whom he could attract into the faith, and had continued to live like a confessor to some Spanish monarch, while dressing in the old accoutrements of an Anglican clergyman, with a wide-rimmed clerical hat, stockings held at the knee with gaiters, and a black frock coat over a silk waistcoat and purple shirt.'[8]

I ask Scruton to tell me a little more about Monsignor Gilbey. 'I found him so amusing. He was an extraordinary survival from the eighteenth century. He astonished me with the completeness of his Catholic faith, as set out in his book *We Believe*. That is, to me, the best statement of the ordinary doctrine of Catholicism. He lived by it completely, and radiated a kind of certainty that I have never seen in anybody else. You don't see it in Anglican clergymen, let's face it! For them, everything is doubt and worry and incompleteness, whereas Gilbey was buttoned-up and serene. Of course, there were aspects of him that were very dubious. His homosexuality was only *just* under the surface; you felt that it could easily burst out at any time and might be very destructive of the life that he had so meticulously constructed, and in defiance of it.'

It has often been asked of me why Scruton never converted to Catholicism. For this is a man who, despite his love of England and its established church, always seemed to be more at home in the Catholic faith. Indeed, his cultural outlook – and to some extent his political perspective – have been shaped by the aesthetic and sacred norms of Roman Catholicism. He has even written of the Mass, 'with its moment of "transubstantiation"', as a 'decisive experience'. That is because 'it provides us with so persuasive an example of embodied meaning'.[9] And so I ask him why, in spite of all this, he has remained faithful to the Anglican Communion. 'I am actually very cosmopolitan. My soul was, from the first encounter, wrapped up in the idea of France. When I first went there as a boy, I thought it was an enchanted place. French language and literature have always been important to me. During my year there, I absorbed the Balzacian Catholicism of rural France and it seemed to me something very beautiful. So I lingered on the edge of the Catholic faith during all the time of my first marriage. There was no suggestion of being an Anglican then at all, but after divorce it all drifted away. What appealed to me in the Catholic Church were precisely those things that were destroyed by the Second Vatican Council. Before that, I had the sense that this was the ongoing manifestation of something unchangeable and permanent, but not now.'

For anyone who has read *Our Church*, Scruton's passion for the Church of England is not in doubt. That was something I had seen for myself on Palm Sunday. However, I remind him that the Church is dwindling, that many more people go to Sunday Mass and to Mosque than attend Sunday service. So how does he see the future of this Church to which he eventually returned, as he once put it, 'no longer as a thief but as a penitent'? 'I don't know is the simple answer to that. It could be that there will be a revival – maybe an evangelical revival. It is quite surprising how much the evangelical movement has progressed, especially among young people living in the cities. The Church has wonderful institutional structures that keep it in being. It's like the Monarchy: you don't need a monarch for the Monarchy to exist. It goes on as a vacant office and I can see the Church of England going on in that way for a very long time. I can see it filling up again and then emptying again.

'Ultimately, it all depends upon the history of the nation: if we entered into some conflict, triggered, let's say, by the threat of invasion from Russia, or by mass immigration from an essentially hostile Muslim world, and people really had to take the survival of this country seriously, I think you would find it coming back again. But it is true that all religions live and die, and right now Islam is on the up. And looking back on the Hellenistic period, we have the documented death of the old religions. They weren't monotheistic religions and they didn't require a great deal by way of doctrine and faith. They were purely liturgical – ways of bringing the gods to our side, whoever the local gods might be. Such religions are very vulnerable to social and economic change, invasions and migrations. Conversely, the monotheistic religions have a kind of permanence to them. They make permanence into their fundamental goal. So it is more catastrophic when they decline, as the Christian faith is declining in America, England and most of Europe. But there is no evidence that Christianity is on the decline in Africa or Asia. So, who knows?'

In my book *Moral Matters: A Philosophy of Homecoming*, I say that even liberal societies have an interest in reproducing themselves, but that they cannot do this without the institutional structures – such as the Church – which they seem intent on destroying.[10] Scruton responds that this is 'absolutely true and, of course, it's one reason why we conservatives take hope: conservatives reproduce and liberals don't!'

In his widely acclaimed book *The West and the Rest: Globalisation and the Terrorist Threat*,[11] Scruton attacks militant Islam while simultaneously praising the 'natural piety' of ordinary peaceful Muslims. I suggest that such Muslims, who live out their lives sanctifying the day with prayer, tending to their families and caring for the elderly, practise the very things which we need to rediscover. 'I think that is absolutely true. A good Muslim will lead a prayerful life, a family life, and be devoted to his neighbours and his community. He will also hold many things sacred and will not go through life as though he can just abuse whatever he comes across. Everything is God's work and must be respected as such. That is not just admirable, but in the end necessary. It is very hard for us to recapture such a communal state of mind in our atheist culture.

'Of course, apostasy is forbidden to Muslims and the punishment for it is severe; so it is rare for a Muslim to convert. The Muslim will go through a period of not attending to his faith and maybe living an unsanctified life, but always on the assumption that he'll come back to the faith before he dies. But in so far as a Muslim identifies his faith as outside the community in which he lives, he is a danger to that community. That is why Pakistan had to be created as an independent republic, and why the conflict between Muslim and Hindu in the Indian sub-continent won't go away. It's also why we have problems with Muslims now in Europe, and why it is possible to be a believing Muslim and also the implacable antagonist of those with whom you live side by side under a shared rule of law. But in the original environment from which Islam emerged, it was possible to renounce extremism, and to live in the manner invoked in the *Thousand and One Nights*, on polite terms with God, but acknowledging that he is a very long way away, and may not have noticed that you only half believe in him.'

I ask him if he thinks that women will ultimately be the salvation of Islam. 'Well, certainly Islam regards women as a threat, otherwise it wouldn't conceal them. On the other hand, those young girls who go off to join extremist groups do so because they feel there is no place for a woman in Western society, where they must flaunt their sexuality or be ignored. The girls who travel to join Isis do so because the Muslim way of life offers both to hide them and to protect them.'

Christianity has a corporate personality, has a face that you can talk to and structures that can be held to account, whereas Islam does not. Is this the central problem? 'That is indeed crucial. We inherited the achievement of Roman law in institution building. Sharia law is not addressed to institution building at all. It is addressed to the individual and it says "this is how you must live". I have never heard this question answered by Muslim apologists: where are the institutions and do they have legal personality? Or is the local Imam only ever saying what *he* thinks, which another Imam might spontaneously denounce as heretical? One can still hope that there will be a side-by-sideness of the faiths in this country, as there was for centuries in Lebanon and Syria.'

Is *The Soul of the World* Scruton's definitive statement on these matters, or has he more to say? 'I am sure I shall have more to say in due course, but it is what I've said so far. I'm only feeling my way around the question of religion. But, yes, *The Soul of the World* is my attempt to give a philosophy of what we are, where we are and how we are. And I think it addresses some of the fundamental questions.'

12

Living as a Writer

'I am my ideal reader'

It is afternoon on the final day of our conversations and we return to the question of writing. Earlier, Scruton mentioned that, in the beginning, writing did not come easy to him. I ask him to elaborate. 'I found it very difficult, but have always taken the Protestant view that nothing works like work, and that if you're not succeeding you must try again. I don't have an innate talent; I'm not a spontaneous, creative person. I do, however, have a capacity to work and an ability to synthesize things – I look for images, metaphors, comparisons, try to bring things together and crystallize them in a single thought. This is something I had to work on. As I said, it started coming partly through journalism.'

I have noticed that the very first thing Scruton does each morning is write. When did he commit to writing every day and in this systematic way? 'When I was sixteen, and I haven't stopped since. I didn't know what I was doing, but wanted to be like the great characters whose works I was reading. I knew there was no hope of being like them in reality, but nevertheless thought there might be a pretend version I could aspire to.'

And when did it dawn on him that it was possible to be a writer? 'Not until long after I had left Cambridge, studied for the Bar and had published *Art and Imagination*. That gave me a sense of being intellectually established, but not yet a writer. But, as we have discussed, when I was writing *The Aesthetics of Architecture*, things started flowing in another way. Then I felt, yes, maybe I will be able to write in the long run. In 1979, I went to

Princeton to teach a course on architectural aesthetics and it was there that I wrote the first draft of *The Meaning of Conservatism*. That flowed because I was writing what I meant. But the result was very crude and had to be completely rewritten. Even so I am embarrassed by quite a bit of it now.'

From these conversations, we now know that, in 1981, Scruton wrote *Kant: A Very Short Introduction* in just four days, by which time things obviously were flowing very well. 'Yes, at that time there was a big breakthrough. It was no longer difficult to write, at least philosophical things. On the other hand, writing any kind of evocative essay or fiction was still very hard. Although I had been doing that for quite a while, it took another decade before I was in any way fluent – and even so, I have real difficulties.'

In 1981, as mentioned earlier, Scruton published *A Short History of Modern Philosophy: From Descartes to Wittgenstein*. That book, which is still in print and branded a 'Routledge Classic', is a remarkably lucid synthesis of modern European thought. How did it come about? 'That was a commission from Routledge, who said it would be a very useful book for them to have. I didn't believe them, but the contract came with an advance at a time when I was really short of funds. I found writing the book quite easy because, by then, I had taught much of the material at Birkbeck. I also had my own views on those thinkers. That said, the first edition was very weak on certain philosophers about whom I had to improvise. You cannot summarize a philosopher in ten pages if you haven't spent at least a year studying him. The shorter your summary, the more you need to know. To get the essence of someone like Spinoza is very hard. I had, however, very much enjoyed teaching the history of philosophy, and I had tried to do it in Jonathan Bennett's way, which is to say I tried to *interrogate* historical philosophers rather than repeat what they said.

'That is the strength of the analytical method: you're not in the business of repeating other people, but in the business of holding them to account. It doesn't matter if they are as great as Kant: they still have to answer your questions. That, I think, is a wonderful change in people's approach to the history of philosophy. Bennett was a major influence on me in that respect.'

In 1986, and following from the popularity of his Kant book, Scruton published *Spinoza: A Very Short Introduction*.[1] I wonder if Spinoza is still important to him. 'Yes because he is the model for the kind of "cognitive dualism" that I develop in *The Soul of the World*. He recognized that the scientific view of the world doesn't leave anything out, but, nevertheless, is not the whole truth of the matter. That which is explained from one perspective can also be understood from another, and the two perspectives are incommensurable. He worked this thought out in his extraordinary "two-aspect theory", arguing that theories of mind and extension are two ways of conceptualizing the whole of things. Spinoza had a really scientific mind and didn't in any way want to marginalize science or to isolate the human person from the rest of nature. He wanted to acknowledge the sovereignty of physics, while also limiting that sovereignty, so that the world lying on the dissecting table can also rise up and address us with a smile.'

There is no doubt that writing seems to have become easier for Scruton since he moved to the country. In that time, he has published thirty of his books. Has the tranquillity of this place inspired him? 'To be quite honest, the only tranquillity I ever experience is in London or Washington. Here, you sit down at your desk, look from your window and at once jump up again, crying, "My God, that fox is coming down into the yard and the chickens are out!" or "What's that horse doing in the field?" or "Whose sheep are those?" The countryside is a constant source of anxiety. I will say, however, that after leaving Boston I intended to settle here and make a go of it. My journalism didn't bring in very much, and fees from other things were irregular. Once Sophie and I had married it was clearly necessary to start earning again. Our venture into media relations supported us for a while, at least until the big crash. But it was more and more a matter of urgency to sign contracts with publishers, which meant committing to the kinds of writing that publishers ask for. I am not bestseller material, and have never been able to command much of an advance. Nevertheless I found myself writing for another audience than a classroom of students. So inevitably my style became more accessible, and more personal too. People are not interested in what you write if they do not sense the person behind it.'

For whom, then, was he writing? Did he have an ideal reader? '*I* am my ideal reader and I am writing things I would like to read. I think there are enough people like me and that is really how I see it.'

Scruton, I suggest, places high emphasis on elegant writing. 'Yes, I hate plodding and jarring writing, as you do. I think this is one of the things that put me off the academic world and puts me off academic philosophy. Of course, not all academic philosophers write that way. There are some who write very clearly and agreeably, such as the British philosopher Tim Williamson and the American Tom Nagel. Anscombe's book *Intention* is in its way very stylish. Wittgenstein wrote beautifully, as did Quine, Nelson Goodman and Donald Davidson. Quite a few American philosophers, under the influence of Quine, have cultivated a lapidary style.'

I ask if he thinks it is important to write fiction in order to write properly, to which he quickly responds: 'No. Hobbes and Bacon didn't write fiction, but they wrote better English prose than anybody of their time. My ambition to write fiction was there from the beginning, since I believed that philosophy could be continuous with the life of the imagination. That is why Sartre, Nietzsche and Kierkegaard have been important for me, whether or not I agree with what they are saying.'

So what, then, are the qualities of a great writer? 'A great writer is someone like Tolstoy, Dostoyevsky or Jane Austen, someone who can put himself *completely* into the mind of another person and find the language that will both express and vindicate a way of being that is not his own. That is not an easy thing to do. There are still people writing fiction who try to do this. In Austen's day, although there was eccentricity, the eccentric was continuous with everybody else. He shared the social norms, so his experience could be captured in the same syntax as might be used for the most ordinary things – witness Boswell on Johnson, or Sterne's *Tristram Shandy*. But that is not quite so now: novelists explore the peripheries of social life, but usually using the language that they find there, and not the sculpted syntax that they might reserve for a strait-laced story about strait-laced people.

'It is noticeable that although music, painting and architecture have all gone through a great crisis in the modern period, so that it is not clear what remains of them, fiction has not. Maybe there isn't the great panoramic novel like *Middlemarch* or *War and Peace*, but there are powerful works of fiction which describe the world as it is, which don't sentimentalize and which are genuinely engaging and moving. There has not been the disruption that occurred in the other arts. That is a very interesting fact and I don't know why it is. The attempts at modernist fiction – which is to say, the later Joyce, and post-war preciosities like Maurice Blanchot and the *nouveau roman* – were so many dead ends. Joyce in *Ulysses* did something absolutely wonderful. But it could never be done again. Nor did it really lead to anything, although I am full of admiration for experiments like Georges Perec's *La vie, mode d'emploi* and *La disparition*. But *Finnegans Wake*, in my view, is a kind of cabbalistic tinkering. Not to say that I don't approach that book in a spirit of humility: in Joyce you encounter refined observation and a sensitivity to words that reduce all critical cavils to silence.'

These days, Scruton is often deemed a 'public intellectual'. Is he content with that title? 'In so far as I understand what that is, I suppose I am a public intellectual. That is to say, I don't deny that I am an intellectual and I go public! I would prefer to think of myself as a "man of letters". John Gross's book *The Rise and Fall of the Man of Letters* was very significant.[2] I think he was right that, somehow, this calling has gone. In that respect, I suppose I am now somewhat unusual.'

Of all his books, which is Scruton most proud of and why? 'Being proud of them is one thing and thinking they are any good is another! I am proud of *The Aesthetics of Music* because it took an extremely difficult subject and licked it into shape. Although one might disagree with a lot of it, I suspect that it may be recognized in time. *Xanthippic Dialogues* is one of my favourites, especially the last dialogue, "Phryne's Symposium". That contains the essence of my book *Sexual Desire*, but in the form of jokes. I think that was something of an achievement.'

Where did the idea for that marvellous book, published in 1993, come from? 'Someone asked me to write a little philosophical play to be performed at the Royal Court Theatre. I wrote "Xanthippe's Republic" first because I thought that turning Plato's *Republic* on its head would be a nice way of doing it: my audience would surely know Plato's *Republic* and understand my little play as a response to it. Then I thought, let's do it again by satirizing the entire Platonic worldview from a feminine perspective. For all its faults the result is properly written and makes its point.'

I remark that some serious writers have told me that *Xanthippic Dialogues* not only changed the way they think, but was one of the funniest books they have ever read. As a person who wasn't always known for his humour, Scruton showed in that book that he has a seriously humorous side: 'There has always been a certain amount of humour in what I have written. You find it in *On Hunting* and *News from Somewhere*. *News from Somewhere* is always moving on from one significant detail to another without losing track of itself, and that, at least, is a virtue. I am also quite proud of *Death-Devoted Heart* on Wagner's *Tristan and Isolde*, and also of *The Disappeared*. I think that book is neat! *Notes from Underground* tries to condense a very difficult and complex little bit of the European experience in an unusual way. I guess those books go some way towards justifying the time spent in writing them, though I am always aware of the many ways in which my writings fall short of the ideal.'

Scruton followed *Xanthippic Dialogues* with *Perictione in Colophon*. It is a darker and much more serious work. Why did he choose to go darker? 'I should have been more light-hearted about it. It's a bit over-written at times. It's really trying to take the whole thing forward into the modern world. Yes, it's a darker book altogether, but I enjoyed writing it, as I have all these things. I greatly enjoyed the character of Perictione. I have to say that if I had had the good fortune to be born a woman, I would have tried to be like her.'

This prompts me to ask which, of all the characters he has invented, is his favourite? To my surprise he says Zoë Kostas from his novella *A Dove Descending*, published in 1991.[3] He says rather poignantly: 'I think of her with love. I wrote that story over quite a long time in the Eighties, when I was in a much more lonely condition. I was making up my mind to leave Birkbeck and it contains reminiscences of Birkbeck. Zoë was my first attempt to explore the situation of the immigrant who loves outside her community and is punished for it.'

These days, Scruton seems to move seamlessly between fiction and philosophy. In terms of organization and writing technique, how do they differ? 'Fiction requires much more discipline because the imaginative effort is very hard. When I am working on a piece of fiction, I must really set aside the two hours in the morning when I'm doing nothing else. I don't do the kind of historical research that someone like Hilary Mantel would do because I'm not writing in that way. But with *Notes from Underground* I did investigate the background, even though the central story is based on memory and imagination of my own.

'Regarding composition, I usually write until I get to a certain point and then say, "I'll stop there and start again tomorrow." What determines whether I stop depends on what kind of book I'm writing. With *The Disappeared* it was very clear where I should stop. Something had to be left in suspense. Fiction of that kind is a matter of controlling information: knowing when to withhold it and when to release it.'

The Disappeared is set in a Yorkshire city and is a story of sex trafficking, the tyranny of political correctness, social deprivation, personal ruin and redemption. What struck me when reading it was the way Scruton has detailed daily life in the fictional sink estate of Angel Towers, as well as the vivid descriptions of the seedy underworld of sex slavery and the mind-set of young British Muslim men. This, I suggest, is not the type of world in which you might expect to bump into Roger Scruton. 'No, to put it mildly!' How, then, can someone who is so at odds with that world seem so at home in it? 'I have enough basic information from my own life, and after all it is a work of the imagination. I have acquired some knowledge of the Polish underworld from my experience of Poland. I have knowledge of Muslim ways of thinking and the way of life of Muslim immigrants, and I have thought long and hard about the Muslim view of women. There was much in my own life to draw on and the Honeyford Affair put me straight into the heart of that confrontation in Bradford, which was the beginning of the situation that I describe. I like *The Disappeared* because it fits together like a Rubik's cube.'

Does he think that fiction can convey his message with as much force as his philosophical or political writings? 'It's difficult to judge. Fiction is not there to exhort people, to change their ways or to advance a political programme. When it does try to do that it is always an artistic catastrophe, like the socialist realist novels that came out of Russia in the 1930s. But fiction has a greater capacity than philosophy to show the world as it is. Hegel describes art as the sensuous embodiment of the idea, meaning that art gives to the thoughts that it expresses an immediate and sensory impact. The response to a novel should be, yes, this is how life is. And if you get it right, then you don't only produce that response; you also elicit sympathy for your characters. This is not like an exhortation, a propaganda invocation to go out and change the world. It is a way of offering your readers emotional knowledge, putting them in touch with possibilities that might otherwise have remained hidden.

'Sympathy comes through novels, poetry and theatre, in a way that it doesn't come through philosophy. That is because you have specific people to sympathize with. Their predicament comes across to you, in part, as yours. That is what Sartre achieved with *La Nausée*. In my view Sartre's novel is not a great work of art since the central character, Roquentin, is empty, a kind of nothingness, a mere vehicle for an abstract idea. Nevertheless, by putting this nothingness in fictional form, Sartre persuaded a generation of Frenchmen to see their predicament in the run-up to the Second World War in metaphysical terms. A movement of self-understanding began there, which changed the culture. For Sartre, the work of fiction describes the world as though it were the expression of an act of freedom. The world in fiction is no longer just a brute fact, but a moment of free creation. So, in a sense, fiction automatically gives the God's-eye view of things. This is what makes Sartre such a great literary figure and it is a tribute to France that so many people thought that his death marked the end of an era and a moment of real cultural loss.'

Apart from Sartre, who are Scruton's favourite writers? 'In fiction, I guess Flaubert, Chekhov, Joyce, Dostoyevsky, Tolstoy, and I think very highly of Zola, and Dickens at his best, as in *Great Expectations* (though with the original ending). Among my contemporaries, I think highly of Ian McEwan and Edward St Aubyn as well as the poets Don Paterson and Ruth Padel, among many others. It has to be recognized that much modern literature has given up on the task of engendering sympathy, and stretching that sympathy as far as it will go. In *Crime and Punishment* Dostoyevsky takes a murderer and gets inside him, and you the reader are inside him too. That is an extraordinary achievement. There is much literature that gives immorality more time than it deserves. Baudelaire, for example, relishes the seediness of life, but in language that evokes an inaccessible world of purity and beauty. It is a paradox that Baudelaire puts before us, and he set an example that lesser writers – and all of us are lesser writers than Baudelaire – ought to be wary of following.

'If a work of art *merely* evokes seedy and disgraceful things, and has no compensating vision of redemption, then it has no aesthetic merit either. The Marquis de Sade illustrates this. His writings are a complete flop, without real characters, the sentiment laid on with a trowel. Their huge influence in France is due to their subject-matter alone. The big question is whether, *through* beauty, immorality can be redeemed or rescued, and, if so, is that a bad point for beauty, or a good point for immorality? That is a question I am really interested in, but I haven't an answer to it.

'What I can say is that all drama appeals to our sympathies and we can only be interested in it to the extent that we can be on the side of a given character, and also fearful on his or her behalf. In fiction you are educating your sympathies. That is one reason why storytelling has been a human universal: it is one way in which young people come to understand that there's a world larger than themselves.'

Isn't it true that television and film can serve to provide, for the current generation, the same sort of emotional training as literature did for ours? 'Oh yes, I think we have to accept that a new human type is emerging, for whom information is primarily taken in through the screen and not through reading or reciting. That is true, but it doesn't follow that they're not absorbing from their sources the kind of things that we absorbed from books.'

Is this decline in the literary culture as serious as the decline of the religious culture? 'It's the same phenomenon, I believe, because what the religious culture did for us was to make us into "people of the Book", as Muhammad put it. He wanted his people to have a book and so he presented them with one – a dreadful mistake in this particular case. With the decline of religion, the importance of the book, as the entity that opens the door into another world, is vanishing. For someone like me, the decline of the literary culture is a deep cause of sadness because that is how I have lived. It is not just how I earn money, but the book defines what I want to be and what I want to belong to. To belong to something that is disappearing is not a happy condition.'

Does he have a specific writing routine? 'Not really. I get up in the mornings, go straight to my desk and start writing. If it goes well, I could be engaged in it for the rest of the morning. If it doesn't, I'll go and muck out the horses. However, there is always a period in the day when I'm hard at it. When writing a book, I am always anxious to have a completed draft so that I know where I'm going. And that's what I increasingly do now: instead of going slowly, I go rapidly to the end and then begin again from the beginning, tearing it up as I go.'

What advice has Scruton got for aspiring writers? 'The most important thing is patience. You are not to worry that you've spent the whole day writing and there's nothing to show for it. There *will* be. And even if there is just one sentence that you are pleased with, that is better than no sentences. The other piece of advice is that you shouldn't be taken in by some vision of yourself as a "creative artist". Forget that and remember that you are just an ordinary human being labouring in the vineyard. You have got your task in front of you and you must try to do it well. Oscar Wilde wrote in a letter, "I spent the morning working on the proof of a poem and took out a comma. In the afternoon I put it back again." Thus speaks the craftsman. And craft really matters – see Percy Lubbock's helpful book, *The Craft of Fiction*.'

And what advice would he give left-wing writers? 'Acknowledge the legitimacy of disagreement.'

13

Making Music

'I can't live without creating'

We have touched on music at many points in our conversations, but as we approach the end I want to ask Scruton about his lifelong interest in composing. When did he first begin composing? 'I did a little bit of composing in my teenage years, when I was fourteen or so. However, around 1987 or 1988, when I was on the verge of leaving Birkbeck, I wrote a libretto for an opera called *The Minister*, which is a one-act lyrical drama in which an aspiring politician encounters the ghosts of the two people whom he has most deeply betrayed. I asked various composer friends if they wanted to set it to music and they weren't interested. So I thought, "Why don't I try?"

'I was having a bad time in the wake of *Thinkers of the New Left*. Everything I wrote was rubbished, and although I was still publishing books I began to think that I should give up writing. Perhaps I wasn't doing the thing I should be doing. That is when I moved to the country cottage just outside Swindon. I moped for a bit, but quickly understood that I can't live without creating. So I sat down at the piano and began inventing things, setting some of the words of my libretto to music. Then it started coming.

'I wrote a full draft of *The Minister* and showed it to the composer David Matthews, who is a close friend. He said that it wasn't entirely bad, that I had the bass-line and other things that people don't always think about. So I asked him if he would give me lessons and he eagerly accepted, in exchange for lessons in philosophy. After that, I rewrote *The Minister* and completed a performable version. I also composed some Lorca songs and a few piano pieces. Then Jessica Douglas-Home found a little group of students in Oxford whom she paid to perform the opera in her house, in a version for four singers, two pianos and keyboard, as a fiftieth birthday present for me. Some of it (though by no means all of it) sounded perfectly acceptable!

'The orchestral version of *The Minister* had a few more performances, including one in Oxford that was well received and was even reviewed in *The Times*. It hasn't been put on properly since. Later Jessica wrote a biography of her great-aunt Violet Gordon Woodhouse, who joined Arnold Dolmetsch in introducing the early music movement to England. Violet led a stunning life, changing mid-career from a romantic pianist to a cute and man-killing doll at the harpsichord. I was very impressed by her character, as Jessica described it. Jessica also made a little theatrical tableau out of the book, in which an actor presented critical moments in Violet's life while Maggie Cole filled in the background at the harpsichord. I said to myself that it would work even better as an opera. This occurred at another of the bleak periods of my life, when I had again lost confidence in the future. My daily task, then, was to turn Jessica's biography into a libretto, and having done that to compose the music.

'The resulting two-act opera impressed the late Julian Hope, who was a friend of Jessica's and well connected in theatre and music circles. Julian and Jessica persuaded Clive Timms at the Guildhall School of Music to put together a suitable cast and rehearse the work for production. The opera has had the one outing, consisting of two performances at the Guildhall. But it was properly done and the young performers projected everything beautifully. You can find the result on the web.'

Scruton has regularly confided in me that he finds composing difficult, but surely it is a different type of 'difficult' to his fictional writing or philosophy? 'That is true: I am not a natural composer. I am also not the only person who creates in different media. Arrigo Boïto, who wrote the libretti for Verdi's great operas, also wrote operas of his own. One of them, *Mefistofele*, is still in the repertoire and it is a very important work. Rousseau also composed an opera, *Le devin du village*. Although I do not share Rousseau's great talent and literary genius, I am a bit like him in that I bring philosophy, fiction and music together in my work. That said, I would like to think that if Rousseau saw where his philosophy has led to, he would be more of my persuasion than his own. And *Le devin du village*, although it was popular in its day, is now justly neglected. In literature he turned everything he touched into gold. Not so in music.'

Has he any plans to compose a new opera? 'I have written a libretto for an opera set in a railway station. At the end of my little film *Why Beauty Matters*,[1] we inserted a performance of Pergolesi's *Stabat Mater* in St Pancras railway station. It created a lovely atmosphere, and people stopped to listen in wonder and astonishment. It gave me the idea for an opera incorporating the Great Western Railway Band, which performs sometimes in Paddington Station on a Friday evening. I have written some of the music, and maybe someday I might turn back to it.'

We have discussed Richard Wagner's influence on Scruton's philosophy of the sacred, but when did he first encounter his music? 'It was at Cambridge. I fell into the circle of Wagnerians there around Michael Tanner, who was and is a great proselytizer for Wagner. He made it clear to the undergraduates who came within his sphere of influence that we had to listen to Wagner, otherwise we would not count as real human beings. Wagner's music is art at its most majestic and ambitious, and a vindication of art as a way of life. At the time, I was reading Thomas Mann, who tried to put in plain German prose what Wagner had given us in music. Both men tried to give a complete vision of civilization and of the modern consciousness as its bewildered heir. Thomas Mann was one of the few artists who had an intellect on the same level as Wagner's. In *The Magic Mountain*, *Dr Faustus* and *Joseph and his Brothers* there is a persuasive vision of the grandeur of human life, and of the temptations that beset us, now that our spiritual inheritance has been squandered.

'By the time I reached Cambridge I had a complete map of Western music. There was a wonderful music section in High Wycombe town library from which I could borrow the classics and play through them with my friend down the road. We knew everything, or could guess everything from performances on the radio. Wagner's music was therefore by no means new to me. However I quickly came to understand that I had never heard it in its full context. Tanner used to invite groups of us to listen to a full

Wagner opera, on equipment that was very advanced for its day. That was a great experience. I became fascinated by *Tristan and Isolde*, a work built around a single integral experience, a translation into seamless melody of a metaphysical conundrum that could not be put into words. My interest in *Tristan* set me on the phenomenological path. Such art presents what is otherwise inner, hidden and known only to the one who suffers it. It translates the subjective into the objective so that the subjective can be shared. You can hear this magic accomplishment in the very first bars: here is a mystery, they tell us, and here too is the key to it.'

But surely Scruton got the idea of the subjective mystery of things from Kant and not Wagner? 'Yes, except that *Tristan* offered a real example. Kant talks about the aesthetic ideas, but in a way that is completely detached from the specifics of artistic creation. It was so clear that Wagner was making *whole* what was otherwise fragmented in our experience. I felt this very strongly with *Tristan* and found it also in *Die Meistersinger*. There, he is giving the subjectivity not of an individual but of a community – something that has not elsewhere been attempted, except in the same composer's more mystical *Parsifal*.

'After Cambridge I drifted away and only came back to Wagner in the mid-Eighties when I was at Stanford on a Hoover Fellowship. I began to study *The Ring*, working out the leitmotifs and writing little things about it. I published a few papers here and there and then, in 2004, *Death-Devoted Heart*. By then, I had found a language with which to describe Wagner's artistic aims and the methods used to achieve them.'

I persist with the question: however original Wagner's take on all this, wasn't it true that he took it straight from German idealism and Kant in particular? 'German idealism got Wagner started, but you have to remember that there was another current of opinion in late eighteenth-century Germany. From Herder and the brothers Grimm came the idea that the *Volk* reveals its collective soul in legend and myth. Wagner's original artistic inspiration arose from two sources: the romantic nationalism of Herder and his followers, and the philosophy of the free individual developed by Fichte and Hegel, and then given a political and materialist makeover by Feuerbach. The post-Kantians were largely of a mind, wanting to use Kantian philosophy as the foundation for a national culture, one that would fill the void left by the fading of the Christian religion. Wagner was fascinated by Jacob Grimm's attempt to trace myths and language to their shared source in the consciousness of a people: like Grimm he was looking for hidden messages and buried treasure, and in a way Lévi-Strauss was right to describe Wagner as the founder of structural anthropology. Once you bring all those ideas and interests together you've essentially got *The Ring*.'

One of the most striking things about Wagner, I suggest, is that he was someone who not only composed but who wrote serious philosophy and also fiction. 'Yes, he was a very remarkable man. I gave some lectures in 2006 at Princeton on *The Ring* and read many of Wagner's literary works around that time. I have to say that they are difficult, written in a hectic style, often ungrammatical and just pouring out without sequence. You get the sense that he wrote as he talked. He was a dominating personality who snatched words from others as they were trying to utter them, only to throw them back in great clusters of annihilating emotion.'

Currently, Scruton is writing a book on Wagner's *Ring* for Penguin. I ask him to give me his take on this epic cycle of operas. 'In my view *The Ring* contains a true vision of the moral order. It shows the modern world as it really is – as a spiritual bequest that we can retain only subjectively, and without the benefit of a shared religion. It does this through an extraordinary drama, but also through the music, which picks up all the inner meanings of the external action. That is Wagner's great achievement. Those inner meanings are there in you and me, whereas the action is not. It is precisely because the action takes a mythological form, involving gods and heroes whose situation is remote from ours, that it creates a vehicle for a universal meaning, and arouses in us feelings that are becoming fully conscious for the first time.'

The other great composer who often features in Scruton's work is Beethoven. In particular, the late quartets have exerted a lasting influence. Why is this? 'I don't think there's a specific message there, except that Beethoven is, for me, what he has been for just about everybody who has ever listened to him. He is the paradigm of artistic dedication, the one who is not just totally immersed in his art, but who puts into his art everything that he is and the vision of the world that comes from being what he is. His work is a labour of sacrifice and, at the same time, an impeccable invention. It is immediately attractive and appealing, and yet also elusive and deep. This is just an extraordinary combination of qualities and you sense enormous suffering working its way towards its own artistic resolution. One has the same experience with Schubert too, but it was Beethoven who made Schubert possible. The "late" Schubert quartets – he wrote them when he was only half your age! – were as innovative as the late Beethoven quartets.'

When sitting down the road with his friend in High Wycombe, did Scruton discuss music and the great composers as we are discussing them now? 'No. He was the first encounter I had with a real musician. He couldn't say anything about the music he loved, since for him all words were superfluous. He would show you what a piece of music meant by playing it. Philip Saudek was his name. His grandfather, who was a student of Freud in Vienna, was a graphologist who applied the psychoanalytic method to the study of handwriting. His father was a surgeon who, like Philip, saw little need to communicate to anyone except his children. And he would communicate with his recorder. He knew the entire repertoire and he would sit in the kitchen listening to the radio while playing his recorder in unison with whatever symphony was being broadcast, choosing now this part now that through the whole range of the score. As he played he would raise and contract his eyebrows, looking across the octaves of musical space into the eyes of his children. He did not believe very much in any other form of communication and had refused to allow his children to acquire a gramophone, insisting that they must play music for themselves. His elder daughter (with whom I was in love at the time, though she never returned my feelings) played the clarinet in a similar way, as did Philip the violin, which was his real instrument and which became his profession. At the piano Philip was the servant of the score and a wonderful teacher, from whom I learned by osmosis and without the benefit of a single word.'

Throughout my stay, Scruton has played Wagner consistently on the piano in his study. Does he play like this every day? 'I've not played for a long time, but I have started again just to play through *The Ring*.' Does he listen to music every day? 'Yes, on the radio. I rarely make the effort to put something on the CD player. It is all in my memory and that distracts me. I am not quite like Brahms who, when someone invited him to *Don Giovanni*, pointed to his head and said: "I've got a much better performance in here." I'm not like that, but there is a little bit of that in me.'

What are the pieces that Scruton simply cannot live without? 'I would say *all* of Schubert's songs but especially *Winterreise*; the Mozart operas and, as you mentioned, the Beethoven quartets; the late Wagner operas and all of Bach, but most especially the *St Matthew Passion*.' I interrupt to ask if, this being Holy Week, he will listen to this last piece? 'It's an interesting point … Either that or *Parsifal* has always been my Good Friday listening. But regarding my favourite pieces, I would have to add the Stravinsky ballets. These are an immovable part of my education, and a source of unremitting joy.'

What of his favourite contemporary composers? 'I think James MacMillan is very talented. To me, his large-scale orchestral compositions seldom work, but things like his meditation on the *Seven Last Words from the Cross* are most beautiful. There, he displays a melodic and harmonic gift within the constraints of modernism – which forbids old-fashioned cadences but which does not prevent MacMillan from achieving a haunting melodic line. I think there are many English composers writing now who are really very good: David Matthews, Robin Holloway, Oliver Knussen, Judith Weir and many others. Some of them make barbaric sounds, but most have worked their way through to the other side of modernism, where the human voice can once again be heard.'

I suggest that there really is a need for the resurrection of melody. 'Yes and I think this is especially true in opera. I've been discussing this with the composer Ryan Wigglesworth lately, because he has been working on a setting of *The Winter's Tale*. So much modern opera is beautifully crafted noise, which sends you into spasms and may be very evocative. However, the vocal line in front of the noise is mere recitative: it never takes off, never soars, never takes you out of speech into the world of song. Many composers now hesitate to write melodies, thinking that melodies are kitsch. If you try to make a melody, you will immediately drop to the level of the musical. But that level is not so very bad! Stephen Sondheim, Cole Porter and Richard Rodgers were people with genuine talent and occasional touches of genius.'

For so much of its history, classical music was defined by melody, so why does he think it fell so dramatically out of favour? 'Adorno writes about this in an often quite illuminating way. As we know from the theory of addiction, when you trace a psychic path towards pleasure again and again the path becomes a groove: it can no longer be resisted and an addiction sets in, driving on to the reward irresistibly, but with ever diminishing ability to provide it. Something similar happens in music, and when it happens the pleasurable sequence becomes a cliché, like the twelve-bar blues or Chopsticks. Adorno felt that this had happened with tonality generally. After too much use tonality stands as an open door into musical kitsch. Chord progressions become mechanical devices, which merely repeat themselves. Melodies no sooner begin than they settle into the rut that takes them, independently of themselves, to a banal conclusion. To find a melody that doesn't do that is hard. Hence Schoenberg proposed a completely new way of constructing melodies, so that they are lifted out of the ruts. The problem is that no one hears them as melodies, even if some pretend to do so.'

It is, of course, very important that we recreate a classical climate in music, but surely no ordinary person who hears anything by Schoenberg could be weaned onto classical, for the reason that Schoenberg doesn't have the capacity for melody as traditionally conceived? Scruton agrees: 'That is true of his atonal works, though of course everybody loves *Verklärte Nacht*.' And do we really have to worry so much, especially in a time of crisis when so few are listening to classical music, whether melodies are perceived by aficionados as kitsch or not? Surely the important thing is to get people listening to melodies again and then to take things from there? 'I think Adorno and his generation were right to be wary of kitsch. It's not like a false progression or a wrong note – a mere mistake of grammar. Kitsch is a deep aesthetic fault and the ruination of the artistic enterprise. It takes us out of the world of real feeling into that of sentimentality and pretence. In a real sense, it cannot be art, since it cannot perform the only task that makes art worthwhile.

'Adorno had a question, and it is one that T. S. Eliot also had concerning literature, which is this: why is it that these melodic forms and harmonies were not just natural in Mozart's day, but the expressions of real and committed social emotions, whereas if you use them now, they are not? I think that is a perfectly legitimate question. Similarly, following Eliot, you could ask of Walter de la Mare: why is this idiom, which was so raw and heart-searching in Tennyson, now so escapist and remote from the world in which we live?'

But surely a person can still be redeemed by art of the de la Mare kind? 'Of course, there is a severe way of saying what Eliot and Adorno say which might elicit the response you've just given. There is, however, a mild way of saying it, which leads to a serious question: how are we going to rectify these mannerisms that lapse so constantly into escapism and kitsch? How are we to purify the dialect of the tribe, as Eliot says, borrowing from Mallarmé? All composers have felt this. Gershwin took over the jazz idiom, cleansed it and, by a stroke of genius, imbued it with the spirit of counterpoint, much as Stravinsky did in the piano concerto. Very few people have been able to emulate that kind of aesthetic renewal, but each person must attempt it.'

I suggest it is the likes of James MacMillan who are leading people back, not only to culture, but also to faith. And they are doing so by resurrecting polyphony, but also the purest form of melody. 'That is all true, but going back and picking up where we left off, so to speak, is never a possibility. In art, doing the same thing again is always doing something else, and if you do the same thing again without *knowing* that you are doing something else then the result is banal. How to do the same thing again and make it truly your own – that is very difficult, the enterprise explored by Borges in "Pierre Menard, Author of *Don Quixote*". But you feel like that when you are composing, especially if you're composing in the idiom of Bach or Mozart. The question is: how can I do this and make it mine, and if I can't make it mine, am I not simply producing pastiche?'

Are there any people currently composing who have managed to recreate serious melody without taking the path of Schoenberg? 'Yes, as you said James MacMillan is one, Robin Holloway too is often very melodic, as is

David Matthews, especially in his recent quartets, the 12th especially. My friend Oliver Rudland has an opera, *Pincher Martin*, which I introduced to an audience in London the other day, which contains a very striking melody – a straightforward melody in B Flat Minor, which somehow takes the opera forward into the inner world of the protagonist in a compelling way. Oliver calls it a "meme", thinking of Richard Dawkins' theory of mental infection.'

And what of classical music more generally: does it have a future in the era of the iPod? 'I'd like to think it does, yes. I've been writing about this on futuresymphony.org, and it has become a personal preoccupation. It is life and death for those at the Future Symphony Institute, whose one concern is that the symphony orchestra and the culture surrounding it should survive. Young musical people introduced to classical music do see its point, especially if they play music together. Making music together is a fundamental experience, and already half of the point of music is lost on young people today because they have no experience of playing it. So yes, we may be losing classical music, but that is not an argument for not working hard to retain it.'

What advice would Scruton offer to aspiring musicians and composers? 'To aspiring composers, I would say never forget melody and learn harmony and counterpoint, even if you don't ever use them. To musicians, I would say learn to play from memory, which alas I never did. The second thing is to play *everything*: play Baroque, classical, modern, jazz, musical and pop songs, so that you know all the modes of enjoyment.'

This reminds me that, despite his often disparaging views of pop music and the culture surrounding it, Scruton also sees redeeming moments in certain types of pop. 'Oh yes, all pop musicians love the music they perform, but they also hate judgement. When I have taught this sort of thing, my first concern has always been to get the students to realize that there is a distinction between the good stuff they listen to and the bad. I have great affection for the Beatles and Elvis, both of whom dominated my youth. The Beatles had a serious melodic gift and also a real grasp of harmony. In the last chapter of *The Aesthetics of Music*, I take the example of *She Loves You* just to show a melodic line in the idiom of pop which explores neighbouring keys in the way that Schubert might.' Who does he believe was the real genius among the Beatles? 'I think Paul McCartney. Obviously, John Lennon had a poetic imagination which was also very useful to them.'

And why Elvis? 'It is the sheer musicianship, the ability to use the voice to create a melodic and rhythmical pulse of its own. There were others of that generation, like Chuck Berry, who were equally natural musicians. Going further back we encounter the true classics of jazz, who worked with post-romantic harmony as well as standard chord sequences. Duke Ellington is the great example, though Art Tatum and Charlie Parker had some of the same comprehensive understanding of tonal space. Ellington had a sure grasp of what music is and what it is capable of. I don't go along with Christopher Ricks in judging Bob Dylan to be a major poet. I think he was a romantic whose melodies are often weak and indecisive. His strummed harmonies are not always related to each other as they should be. But there is a strong persona that comes across all the same.

'I write about Heavy Metal in *The Disappeared* because the character Justin is taken up by it. Metal is very peculiar, but also very serious. The followers of Heavy Metal really do want to make a distinction between the good stuff and the bad stuff, between the stuff that has something to say and the stuff that says nothing.'

14

Acceptance

'I am perfectly accepted now'

In 2004, ten years after leaving Boston, Scruton returned to the United States to make a new home in Rappahannock County, Virginia. How did that come about? 'From around 2000 to 2004, life was difficult. We were newly married and full of hope, but also beaten down by the attacks and, following the collapse of our little consultancy business, financially insecure. And then, when we were at a very low point, the ban on hunting came in. We were convinced we were going to lose the principal thing around which we had built this farm and our shared way of life. It looked as though the community to which we belonged was about to be swept away, and we didn't want to witness this.

'It was at that moment that I got an e-mail from Alan Zuschlag, who had worked at the World Bank and had set himself up on a little farm in Virginia. He had been reading *On Hunting* and my regular column on countryside matters in *The Financial Times*. He wrote to me, slightly facetiously, asking for advice on how to name chickens. We built up a friendship by e-mail and he suggested that we come to Virginia, where the right to hunt is protected under the constitution of the Commonwealth.

'At the same moment, Justice Doug Ginsburg, who is Chief Judge of the Court of Appeals for the District of Columbia, and a professor of law at George Mason University in Arlington, had also been reading *On Hunting*. He wrote to say: "Come on over and I'll show you around." We met Doug in the village of Sperryville by the signboard that says "Antique Tables Made

Daily"! Behind that very American sign we found a very English landscape: a parcel of Old England in the Appalachian foothills.

'Surely, we thought, in the position we had found ourselves, the wise thing would be to leave England and start again from scratch, in a place of new opportunities. I had a circle of supporters in America, and I might be able to find a job, who knows, in a think-tank or a liberal arts college. Then two unexpected events settled the matter for us. First, one of Sophie's aunts died, leaving her a little cottage by the sea on the Isle of Wight. It was a modernist horror in the plush Alain de Botton style, reeking of that awful commodity he calls "happiness", and there was nothing we could conceivably do with the thing save put it at once on the market. And then, just as we had made that decision, an e-mail came from Alan Zuschlag, telling us that he had decided to start a real estate agency and that, as chance would have it, he had a property that would suit us perfectly – an old plantation house from 1745 that had not been lived in for twenty years. It needed work, but was being sold with 175 acres for the price of the land. He added, "If you agree to buy it by 5 o'clock this afternoon I can get it for you. Otherwise it will be too late."

'Well, you can imagine what an anxious day that was. But after making phone calls and sending e-mails all day we discovered that we could mortgage Sunday Hill Farm and the newly acquired modernist cottage for a combined sum that would just meet the asking price for the house in Virginia – Montpelier, Sperryville, photographs of which you can find on the web. We became prospective owners of Montpelier at 5 o'clock that afternoon.'

I interrupt to ask if they ever seriously discussed selling Sunday Hill Farm. 'Well, we thought we might have to, yes. Although we love this place, if things in England were going to be as bad as they looked, why stay? But it is true we did what we could to live in Virginia without selling this place; and one thing we learned from our period of exile is that Sunday Hill Farm is where we belong. Meanwhile, however, we wanted to make a go of it in Virginia. We arrived in Sperryville on a lovely September day and sat on the porch of the beautiful but empty house, unable to believe that it was ours, and staring across the pasture at the wooded hills of what was to become, for us, a much loved landscape. The house had no electricity or water, but there was a tiny cabin attached to it that had both commodities. As we debated our condition, clinging to each other like two trembling monkeys in a cage, a beautiful red fox walked at a leisurely pace across the pasture, as though inviting us to stay. So we stayed.

'It took us six years to restore the house, furnishing it with authentic American antiques, which had been made (daily, no doubt) around our local town of Culpeper for a century or more. Restoration work is difficult in rural America, as indeed is everything else. You may have to travel fifty or a hundred miles for a tile, or a light fitting. But we had the good fortune to be adopted by a hillbilly, Roger Grimes, who had provided us with the bluegrass band for our initial party for the neighbouring rednecks. Roger's brother, Marvin, was in the habit of working through the winter in order to live wild in the woods in the summer, hunting bears and trying his luck with the local women. Marvin called on us and said, "I'm pretty good, so you should take me on. You can get Roger for fifteen bucks an hour. I charge twenty-five because that's what I am worth." And indeed he was. He worked twenty hours a day to the sound of a Christian rock station, hammering, drilling and singing, until the job was done.

'I have always led my life as a high-risk venture, on the understanding that risks are in general rewarded, provided you also take the penalties that come with them. Very soon after making the decision to come to Virginia, when I was living for the most part alone there, in the tiny cabin which was the only habitable part of our vast estate, I began teaching at a little Catholic graduate school for the training of psychologists – the Institute for the Psychological Sciences in Arlington, next to Washington – whose Dean, Gladys Sweeney, I had met in London. Gladys was able to persuade one of her donors to provide me with a professorial salary. I also discovered that the train from New Orleans to Washington could be encouraged to stop (usually three or four hours behind schedule) at Culpeper, where I could park the car.

'So I began to commute to Washington in order to teach the graduates – good Catholics who radiated the Pauline virtues of faith, hope and charity – at the Institute in Arlington. Several of them have remained close friends of mine, and of Sophie too. And teaching at that little school, learning to be more humble in my dealings with people and more circumspect in my opinions, was a real help to me. In the end the only sure response to hurtful accusations from others is to make better, more accurate and less malicious accusations oneself. My teaching duties and my students brought me into contact with what Kierkegaard called "works of love", and helped me to understand that humility and penitence are both parts of love. My days in that little Institute brought to mind the words of the eighty-fourth psalm: "I would rather be a doorkeeper in the house of my God than dwell in the tents of the wicked." I felt that I was beginning to live in another and better way. But it was a hard time for Sophie, for whom the American countryside offered little that would enable her to be fully at home there, and who had no reason to come to Washington.

'The Institute had been set up by the Legionaries of Christ, a new lay order founded in Mexico by someone called Father Maciel, who had a considerable following in Latin America. Unfortunately, in 2006, Fr Maciel was exposed as a sexual predator, a charlatan and a crook, and the order entered a state of crisis. The Institute acquired a new director, Gladys ceased to be Dean, and I soon found my monthly contract terminated. I was lucky enough to find a position at the American Enterprise Institute, where I worked on the book that was subsequently to be published as *Green Philosophy*, though that position too came to an end after a year, so that by the end of 2009 I was unemployed again, and in a fairly precarious position, with large mortgages on our two houses – Montpelier, Virginia, and Sunday Hill Farm, Wiltshire – and no regular source of income.

'We had not sold the farm in Wiltshire, since it had become more and more clear that our destiny was to return to England. The children had been home-schooled at first – one of the great American initiatives of which I entirely approve. But, after a brief spell in a local school in Rappahannock County, Sophie decided that they should be educated in England, and she returned in order to be with them. We discovered that Mr Blair's vindictive legislation had not done the damage intended, that our hunting community was still intact and that I had been forgotten by the media. After one or two lonely winters in Virginia, one of them snow-bound for six weeks at −20°C,

I too made my way back to England. We now needed desperately to sell the Virginia mansion, at a time when the American property market had collapsed. But once again the risk paid off: Alan found an enthusiastic buyer, and we finally said goodbye to America, with a little money in hand for the school fees.'

Surely, however, there is more freedom and a much more convivial atmosphere for people like Scruton in the United States? 'Yes, it is perfectly respectable to be an intellectual conservative in America, and there is a network of support through magazines like *First Things* and *National Review*. There are also conservative circles in Washington and New York. There is *City Journal*, the Manhattan Institute, the Hudson Institute and think-tanks like the American Enterprise Institute (AEI). There is a constant attempt to present a smiling face and to find things for you to do. AEI is a really intelligent right-wing think-tank, the likes of which we don't have over here, unless you count Policy Exchange and the Centre for Policy Studies, which are low-key affairs in comparison. You can be a conservative in America and feel that you have advanced almost to the edge of being human, like a creature roaming in the outer darkness who occasionally dares to press his face against the window and to show that it is not so different from the faces shining inside.'

Is that because Americans are essentially still a conservative people? 'They, like us, are going through a traumatic transition because of immigration and demographic changes. There is no longer a white Protestant majority. But the white Protestant minority, as it has become, is still very tenacious and very protective of its traditions and its political inheritance. There is certainly more room for somebody like me, and I am not regarded as bonkers or singled out for attack. But even in America, the left are in the business of character assassination if they can do it, and the universities are all on the left and relentlessly ideological.

'In America, friendship is extremely quickly and easily formed. Hence, it is as easily forgotten and moved on from. So you can be very lonely even when you are very popular. On the other hand you can easily be rescued in America. People quickly offer help and it is distinctive of Americans that they take pleasure in other people's success. Europeans only resent success, unless it happens to be their own. That is a major quasi-metaphysical difference between the two cultures.'

I suggest that the major left-wing American intellectuals, such as Ronald Dworkin and Richard Rorty, have never been as destructive to their own inheritance as many of their European counterparts. 'Rorty was a melancholy, gentle figure, not without strong leftist prejudices, who certainly believed himself to be a patriot, representing what was best in his country's tradition of practical and well-meaning social initiatives. Dworkin, on the other hand, was a kind of anti-patriot, someone who looked for the objects of American loyalty in order to disparage them. He had an instinct for old-fashioned decencies, which he would hunt out in their sheltered corners and expose to ridicule.

'Dworkin was like Bernard Williams in believing that *all* conservatives are beneath contempt, and that they show their stupidity by the fact that they don't agree with "us". Other American leftists, like Martha Nussbaum, are capable of accepting the existence of legitimate disagreement about their favourite issues. Outside the universities there are also the more open-minded liberal commentators, like Leon Wieseltier, formerly editor of the *New Republic*, who see leftism as something to be argued in the public square, in conditions of respect towards America and its inheritance. And in Canada there is the remarkable figure of Charles Taylor, the philosopher who has, unsuccessfully but tenaciously, tried to launch a political career on the left, and with whom I have always been friendly.'

In 2014, I gave the plenary lecture at a conference on Scruton in Montreal.[1] The event concluded with a rather robust public debate between Roger and Charles Taylor. Beneath the surface, however, you could detect a sense of mutual respect. Scruton agrees: 'Taylor and I once spent a few days in South Africa together, travelling around the Western coast. I think he's a very clever person who has an imaginative grasp of the issues that also interest me. He comprehends everything and the machine turns over very beautifully. He deserves his reputation, though I wish he didn't write at such length.'

Scruton's own reputation is certainly not what it used to be. After all his twists and turns, he is now a Fellow of the British Academy and the Royal

Society of Literature, which was inconceivable a decade ago. He has a good relationship with many of the younger generation of Conservative MPs and has given the Gifford and Stanton lectures. In the light of all this, has he finally found acceptance in his own country? 'Things have changed radically. To become a Fellow of the British Academy, I had to engineer the deaths of Isaiah Berlin, Bernard Williams, Richard Wollheim and a few others! They all croaked about the same time and the resistance was finally over. The Royal Society of Literature came much earlier and there wasn't the same ideological problem. It is also far more important to me, since it is an award for real writing rather than academic accomplishment. I have been made an honorary Bencher of the Inner Temple, which is a yet more treasured connection, since all my political thinking grows, in the end, from a love for English law, for the Inns of Court and for what the Inns have represented in our culture.'

So you are a kind of establishment figure now? 'Certainly, I am no longer on the margins. But I must say that, before all this, I never thought I was ill-treated. What I was saying was certainly not popular and people were entitled to take exception to it. True, I got depressed, because I didn't think that my work was as bad as the reviewers said. Nevertheless, they were only doing what people do, and I was wrong to be as depressed by the reviews as sometimes I was. And to the extent that the attacks on me were arbitrary, so has the acceptance of me been arbitrary too. These things happen because people don't actually care very much. And to want them to care is a kind of vanity.'

Does the fact that people like him are now listened to give Scruton hope for the future? 'To be listened to by people in the same despondent condition as myself is not very encouraging! But yes, I think the atmosphere is changing. People are waking up to the precarious state of things, and to the fact that nothing – or nothing acceptable – is coming to replace the civilization that they have been so eager to repudiate.'

Especially with recent works like *The Soul of the World*, Scruton's philosophical contribution is also being treated very seriously, and the days of bad reviews are over, it seems? 'I think so. There is no longer the viciousness. It was interesting, for example, that my book *How to Be a*

Conservative was chosen by Labour MP Jon Cruddas as Book of the Year in the *New Statesman*.[2] In fact, all three books that I published in 2014 were named Book of the Year by somebody, which was quite a surprise to me. In the areas that I have made my own – such as the philosophy of music – I am no longer dismissed out of hand. It is still the case that the tone of many reviews is: "He's a conservative, *but*..." That I find very annoying, because people don't bother to find out why I am a conservative and what kind of conservative.'

So with acceptance, however grudging, what does the future hold for Scruton now? 'I have still a way to go, I guess. I hope! I want to settle down for a few years and enjoy what I have – the children, the farm and marriage. But I also regret that I am an under-used asset when it comes to the Tory Party, which, despite my lifelong support for it, prefers to keep me at a distance.'

Apart from the book on Wagner's *Ring*, are there any other things that he wants to get off his chest in the years ahead? 'Last year, I gave some lectures at Princeton on human nature and I would like to develop those, perhaps by including some deeper things on the philosophy of law.'

Are there any more television projects in the pipeline to follow his well-received programme *Why Beauty Matters*? 'The programme on beauty was indeed well received and has been influential in the art world. It has given hope to all the people who simply can't cope with the Damien Hirst and Tracey Emin nonsense. I have wanted to do a television series on what is at stake in architecture. But getting the commission means getting past the censors and I tick all the wrong boxes.'

What would Scruton like his legacy to be? 'I suppose I'd like there to be a few standard works that people discuss, like *The Aesthetics of Music*, *The Aesthetics of Architecture* and *England: An Elegy* – those books which record a particular moment and show people what it was. I don't think my legacy is independent of what I have written. Some of that is durable and some of it is less so. Ever since discovering them as a teenager, Spengler's words have haunted me: "One day", he wrote, "the last portrait of Rembrandt and the last bar of Mozart will have ceased to be – though possibly a coloured canvas and a sheet of notes may remain – because the last eye and the last ear accessible to their message will have gone." Spengler had a penchant for striking exaggerations. But in that observation he was surely right. And if that can happen to Rembrandt and Mozart, who am I to hope for any kind of lasting legacy?'

And is he hopeful for the cause of conservatism generally? 'I'm not very hopeful, no. My only qualification to this is that there is no other cause. Nobody else has anything to offer. On the left there are only negatives: the repudiation now of this feature of our inheritance, now of that. All that conservatism ultimately means, in my view, is the disposition to hold on to what you know and love. And if you don't hold on to what you know and love, you will lose it anyway.'

Afterword

It is mid-afternoon as we prepare to depart from Sunday Hill Farm for Bristol Airport. For three days, Scruton and I have conversed about his life and times, his philosophy, his fiction and his music. Before we leave, however, I have one last question. How, I ask, would he like his epitaph to read? Without a pause he smiles and says, 'It should be on a gravestone in the grounds of All Saints in Garsdon, and it should say: "The Last Englishman: Organist at this Church". Behind the often misunderstood public persona is a man for whom nothing matters more than sanctifying the land he loves by playing music. But does that land still exist? Is Scrutopia a hope or a valediction? It is a question I ponder as we depart this 'old cottage of Cotswold stone', a nowhere which has become somewhere.

Notes

Chapter 1

1   Mark Dooley, *Roger Scruton: The Philosopher on Dover Beach* (London and New York: Bloomsbury, 2009); *The Roger Scruton Reader* (London and New York: Bloomsbury, 2009 and 2011).

2   Roger Scruton, *News from Somewhere: On Settling* (London: Continuum, 2004), p. x.

3   Roger Scruton, *On Hunting* (London: Yellow Jersey Press, 1998), p. 7.

4   Roger Scruton, *Gentle Regrets: Thoughts from a Life* (London: Continuum, 2005), pp. 11–12.

5   Scruton, *Gentle Regrets*, p. 90.

6   Roger Scruton, *England: An Elegy* (London: Continuum, 2006). Jack Scruton features primarily in Chapter Seven, 'English Society', pp. 132–173.

7   Roger Scruton, *Our Church: A Personal History of the Church of England* (London: Atlantic Books, 2012).

8   Roger Scruton, *I Drink Therefore I Am: A Philosopher's Guide to Wine* (London: Continuum, 2009), p. 11.

9   Scruton, *Gentle Regrets*, p. 2.

10   Scruton, *Gentle Regrets*, pp. 3–4.

11   See especially *England: An Elegy*, pp. 27–35.

12   Scruton, *Gentle Regrets*, pp. 85–120.

13   Roger Scruton, *Philosophy: Principles and Problems* (London: Continuum, 2005), pp. 19–20.

14   Scruton, *Philosophy: Principles and Problems*, p. 47.

15   Jonathan Bennett, *Kant's Analytic* (Cambridge: Cambridge University Press, 1966).

16   Roger Scruton, *Art and Imagination: A Study in the Philosophy of Mind* (South Bend: St Augustine's Press, 1974).

Chapter 2

1   Scruton, *News from Somewhere*, pp. 7–8.

2   Roger Scruton, *The Aesthetics of Architecture* (Princeton: Princeton University Press, 1979).

3   P. F. Strawson, *The Bounds of Sense: An Essay on Kant's Critique of Pure Reason* (London: Routledge, 1966).

4   Strawson, *Individuals: An Essay in Descriptive Metaphysics* (London: Routledge, 1959).

5   Roger Scruton, *The Meaning of Conservatism* (South Bend: St Augustine's Press, 1980).

Chapter 3

1   Scruton, *England: An Elegy*, p. 131.

2   Roger Scruton, *The Politics of Culture and Other Essays* (Manchester: Carcanet Press, 1981).

3   Scruton, *The Meaning of Conservatism*, p. 2.

4   'Preface to the Third Edition' of Scruton, *The Meaning of Conservatism* (South Bend: St Augustine's Press, 2002), p. ix.

5   Roger Scruton, *Fortnight's Anger* (Manchester: Carcanet Press, 1981).

6   Roger Scruton, *A Short History of Modern Philosophy: From Descartes to Wittgenstein* (London and New York: Routledge, 1981); *The Palgrave Macmillan Dictionary of Political Thought* (London: Palgrave Macmillan, 1982).

7   Roger Scruton, *Kant: A Very Short Introduction* (Oxford: Oxford University Press, 1982).

8   Roger Scruton, *Fools, Frauds and Firebrands: Thinkers of the New Left* (London and New York: Bloomsbury, 2015). This book was first published in 1985 as *Thinkers of the New Left* (Harlow: Longman, 1985).

9   Scruton, *Thinkers of the New Left*, p. 7.

10   Scruton, *Fools, Frauds and Firebrands*, p. vii.

11   Roger Scruton, 'The Virtue of Irrelevance' in *Untimely Tracts* (London: The Macmillan Press, 1987), pp. 1–2. All of Scruton's columns from *The Times* are collected in this volume.

12   Online review of Mark Dooley, *Roger Scruton: The Philosopher on Dover Beach*.

13   Scruton, *Untimely Tracts*, p. 103.

14   Scruton, 'The Honeyford Case' in *Untimely Tracts*, pp. 137–139.

Chapter 4

1   Simon May, *Love: A History* (New Haven: Yale University Press, 2011).

Chapter 5

1   Roger Scruton, *Notes From Underground* (New York: Beaufort Books, 2014).

2   Roger Scruton, 'Man's Second Disobedience: Reflections on the French Revolution' in *Philosopher on Dover Beach: Essays* (Manchester: Carcanet Press, 1990), p. 224.

3   Scruton, 'Man's Second Disobedience', p. 226.

4   See Roger Scruton, 'The Genesis of A Novel' in *Central and Eastern European Review*, July 10 2015 (ceer.org.uk).

5   Scruton, *Notes From Underground*, pp. 10–11.

6   Geoffrey Bennington and Jacques Derrida, *Jacques Derrida* (Chicago: The University of Chicago Press, 1991), p. 334.

7   Roger Scruton, 'Upon Nothing' in *The Aesthetic Understanding: Essays in the Philosophy of Art and Culture* (South Bend: St Augustine's Press, 1998), p. 286.

8   Jan Patočka, *Plato and Europe* (Stanford: Stanford University Press, 2002).

9   Scruton, *Untimely Tracts*, pp. 231–232.

10   Scruton, *News from Somewhere*, p. 91.

Chapter 6

1   Roger Scruton, *The Classical Vernacular: Architectural Principles in the Age of Nihilism* (Manchester: Carcanet Press, 1994).

2   Scruton, *Untimely Tracts*, pp. 3–4.

3   Scruton, *The Aesthetics of Architecture*, p. 247.

4   Scruton, *The Classical Vernacular*, p. 105.

5   https://www.gov.uk/government/news/20-discount-on-your-first-home-announces-pm.

6   Scruton, *Gentle Regrets*, p. 206.

7   Scruton, *The Meaning of Conservatism*, pp. 29–30.

Chapter 7

1   Roger Scruton, *Sexual Desire: A Philosophical Investigation* (London: Continuum, 2006). First published in 1986.

2   Aurel Kolnai, *Sexual Ethics: The Meanings and Foundations of Sexual Morality* (Farnham: Ashgate, 2005).

3   Roger Scruton, *Death-Devoted Heart: Sex and the Sacred in Wagner's 'Tristan and Isolde'* (Oxford: Oxford University Press, 2004), pp. 119–160. See also, Dooley, *The Roger Scruton Reader*, pp. 99–114.

4   Scruton, *Sexual Desire*, p. 362.

5   Alexandre Kojève, *Introduction to the Reading of Hegel: Lectures on the 'Phenomenology of Spirit'* (Ithaca: Cornell University Press, 1969).

6   Roger Scruton, *The Disappeared* (London and New York: Bloomsbury, 2015).

7   Roger Scruton, *The Soul of the World* (Princeton: Princeton University Press, 2014).

8   See Roger Scruton, 'The Sacred as *Lebenswelt*' in James Bryson (ed.), *The Religious Philosophy of Roger Scruton* (London and New York: Bloomsbury, 2016).

9   Scruton, *I Drink Therefore I Am*, p. 140.

10 Scruton, *Sexual Desire*, p. 357.

Chapter 8

1   See Scruton, 'The North London Polytechnic' in *Untimely Tracts*, pp. 146–147.

2   Roger Scruton, *The Aesthetics of Music* (Oxford: Oxford University Press, 1997).

3   Roger Scruton, *Modern Philosophy: An Introduction and Survey* (London: Pimlico, 2004).

4   Scruton, *Thinkers of the New Left*, p. 8.

5   Scruton, *Philosopher on Dover Beach*, p. 10.

6   Scruton, *Philosopher on Dover Beach*, p. 9.

7   Roger Scruton, *Animal Rights and Wrongs* (London: Continuum, 2006). First published in 1996.

8   Scruton, *Animal Rights and Wrongs*, pp. ix–x.

9   See Peter Singer, *Animal Liberation* (New York: Ecco Press, 2001).

Chapter 9

1   See also Chapter 7, 'Caring for Creation', in Mark Dooley, *Moral Matters: A Philosophy of Homecoming* (London and New York: Bloomsbury, 2015).

2   Anthony Barnett and Roger Scruton (eds), *Town and Country* (London: Vintage, 1999).

3   Roger Scruton, *Xanthippic Dialogues* (London: Sinclair-Stevenson, 1993).

4   Scruton, *On Hunting*, pp. 126–127.

Chapter 10

1   Roger Scruton, *I Drink Therefore I Am*, pp. 4–5.

2   Roger Scruton, 'On White Burgundy' in *Untimely Tracts*, p. 60.

3   Scruton, *I Drink Therefore I Am*, p. 59.

Chapter 11

1   Scruton, *England: An Elegy*, p. 107.

2   Scruton, *On Hunting*, p. 78.

3   Roger Scruton, 'The Return of Religion' in Dooley, *The Roger Scruton Reader*, p. 131.

4   Roger Scruton, *The Face of God* (London and New York: Bloomsbury, 2012).

5   See Søren Kierkegaard, *Either/Or*, trans. Howard and Edna Hong (Princeton: Princeton University Press, 1987).

6 Roger Scruton, *Perictione in Colophon: Reflections on the Aesthetic Way of Life* (South Bend: St Augustine's Press, 2000).

7 Scruton, *Gentle Regrets*, p. 63.

8 Scruton, *Gentle Regrets*, pp. 63–64.

9 Scruton, *Philosopher on Dover Beach*, p. 123.

10 Mark Dooley, *Moral Matters: A Philosophy of Homecoming* (London and New York: Bloomsbury, 2015).

11 Roger Scruton, *The West and the Rest: Globalisation and the Terrorist Threat* (London: Continuum, 2003).

Chapter 12

1 Roger Scruton, *Spinoza: A Very Short Introduction* (Oxford: Oxford University Press, 2002).

2 John Gross, *The Rise and Fall of the Man of Letters: English Literary Life since 1800* (Weidenfeld & Nicolson, 1992).

3 Roger Scruton, *A Dove Descending and Other Stories* (London: Sinclair-Stevenson, 1993).

Chapter 13

1 'Why Beauty Matters' was first aired by the BBC in 2009. It is available to view on vimeo.com.

Chapter 14

1 See Mark Dooley, 'Introduction: Saving the Sacred' in Bryson (ed.), *The Religious Philosophy of Roger Scruton*.

2 Roger Scruton, *How To Be a Conservative* (London and New York: Bloomsbury, 2014).

Index